A COUNTER ARGUMENT TO A NEW YORK BESTSELLER

The Power of Now is LOVE

It's all about Love

Kenneth L Fabbi Publication
Lethbridge, Alberta, T1K 7T9, CANADA
FiveFoldCycle@gmail.com

THE POWER OF NOW IS LOVE Copyright © 2025 by Kenneth L. Fabbi

All rights reserved.

Unless otherwise indicated, all biblical quotations are taken from the Holy Bible, New International Version®, NIV® Copyright ©1973, 1978, 1984, 2011 by Biblica, Inc.® Used by permission. All rights reserved worldwide.

No part of this publication may be reproduced in any form, or by any means, electronic or mechanical, including photocopying, recording, or any information browsing, storage, or retrieval system, without permission in writing from the Author. Kenneth, the author, would welcome your communication at FiveFoldCycle@gmail.com.

ISBN: Paperback: 9781777106676

eBook: 9781777106683

Subjects: *Personal Growth - -*
Spiritual Development - -
Spirituality - -

I. Title   II. Fabbi, Kenneth L.

> With Love comes a time of awaking—it spawns an inflection point in our life...
>
> —Kenneth Fabbi

CONTENTS

Introduction   **Page 1**
    The origin of this book 2
    The truth that is within you 4

Chapter One – You Are Not Your Mind 7
    The greatest obstacle to enlightenment 7
    Prayer of Abandonment 13
    Freeing yourself from your mind 16
    Enlightenment: rising above thought 18
    Emotions: the body's reaction to your mind 19

Chapter Two – Consciousness:
                   The Way Out of Pain 27
    Create no pain in the present 27
    Past pain: dissolving the pain-body 29
    The Story of the Two Wolves 34
    Ego identification with the pain-body 36
    The origin of fear 38
    The ego's search for wholeness 41

Chapter Three – Moving Deeply into the Now 43

Don't seek yourself in the mind 43
End the delusion of time 46
Nothing exists outside the now 47
The key to the spiritual dimension 50
Trusting and understanding God for healing 53
Accessing *The Power of Now* 55
Letting go of psychological time 56
Negativity and suffering have their roots in time 61
Finding the life underneath your life situation 63
All problems are illusions of the mind 67
A quantum leap in the evolution of consciousness 70
The joy of Being 71

Chapter Four – Mind Strategies for Avoiding the Now 75

Loss of now: the core delusion 75
Ordinary consciousness and deep consciousness 75
What are they seeking 76
Dissolving ordinary unconsciousness 79
Freedom from unhappiness 82
Wherever you are, be there totally 86
The inner purpose of your life's journey 92
Accessing the Rivers of Living Waters 93
The past cannot survive in your presence 95

Chapter Five – The State of Presence 99
It's not what you think it is 99
The esoteric meaning of 'waiting' 101
Beauty arises in the stillness of your presence 104
Realizing pure consciousness 107
Christ: the reality of your divine presence 111

Chapter Six – The Inner Body 115
Being is your deeper self 115
Look beyond the words 117
Finding your invisible and indestructible reality 118
Connecting with the inner body 119
Transformation through the body 121
Sermon on the body 124
Before you enter the body, forgive 129
Your link with the unmanifested 131
Slowing down the aging process 133
Strengthening the immune system 134
Let the breath take you into the body 138
Creative use of mind 141
The art of listening 141

Chapter Seven – Portals into the Unmanifested 145
Going deeply into the body 145
The source of that chi 147
Dreamless sleep 149
Other portals 152
Silence 157
Space 157
The true nature of space and time 159
Conscious death 170

Chapter Eight – Enlightened Relationships 173
Enter the now from wherever you are 173
Love/hate relationships 178
Addiction and the search for wholeness 180
From addictive to enlightened Relationships 184
Relationships as spiritual practice 186
Why women are closer to enlightenment 194
Dissolving the collective female pain-body 196
Give up the relationship with yourself 197

Chapter Nine – Beyond Happiness and Unhappiness There Is Peace 203
The higher good beyond good and bad 203
The end of your life drama 208
Impermanence and the cycles of life 209
Using and relinquishing negativity 214
The nature of compassion 216
Toward a different order of reality 218

Chapter Ten – The Meaning of Surrender 225
Acceptance of the now 225
From mind energy to spiritual energy 230
Surrender in personal relationships 232
Transforming illness into enlightenment 234
The Weaver 236
When disaster strikes 237
Transforming suffering into peace 239
The way of the cross 242
The power to choose 244
The last recapitulation: the thesis 246
Ancient Timeless, Spiritual Truths 255
A Prayer 257

Appendix A – Rivers of Living Water 259

Appendix B – The Exchange at the Cross   265

Appendix C – Five Fold Cycle
 – Method Of Healing Personal Hurt 273

Appendix D – Baptism in the Holy Spirit 278

Appendix E – The Art of Forgiveness 287

Footnotes 290

ACKNOWLEDGEMENTS:

You know these publications can't be made in isolation. There are always collaboration and personal sharing between the author, editor, and friends.

Thank you, Eswina, for carefully reviewing this work. Your attention to detail, your copyediting, and your depth in faith have made the work clear, consistent, and cohesive. You are a blessing!

Thank you, Dennis, for reviewing the cover artwork and making it work. I always appreciate your friendship!

The Power of Now Is Love

INTRODUCTION

Who am I to write a counter argument, questioning a very well-known contemporary spiritual teacher like Eckhart Tolle?[1] He has sold over two million copies of *The Power of Now: A guide to spiritual enlightenment.*[2] I have 6 publications... well, let's say... I'm not really well known.

On April 1st, 1984, I had an experience that changed my life. I was traveling with my brother, Dr. Ron Fabbi; we had been at a political gathering in Calgary, Alberta, Canada. Both of us felt let down by the political environment; politics was not going to be our claim to fame.

We stopped in a little town called Fort Macleod and joined in an experience that has marked my life. It was the fifth session of a Life in the Spirit Seminar, where people pray for the 'Baptism in the Holy Spirit.' I found a new wonder that dwelt inside. This presence I had experienced before in life, but I had never been able to put my finger on it. I thought I had extra sensory perception. I had powers. This phenomenon had been there often, showing up in little experiences, but most often, like a fly, I would just flick it away.

The Baptism in the Holy Spirit has led to a transformation in my life. I am now ministering through workshops, conferences, and events, encouraging people to open to the inter-active presence and power of the Holy Spirit and His Gifts. The ministry has opened me to the world of publishing. Some of you may have read my material. There are books and YouTube material on *Healing Life's Hurts*, a book encouraging that *You Can Minister Spiritual Gifts,* a book *Powered by the Gift of Tongues*, a booklet teaching about *Scripture Healing,* and a booklet delving into *Wholeness Through Healing and Forgiveness.*

THE ORIGIN OF THIS BOOK
Most of you have read Eckhart Tolle's book *The Power Of Now.* Off and on, I read portions of it. For years it sat in my pile of books I wished to read. Over Christmas of 2024 I picked it up, and as I read, I became angry! I decided to write a counter argument to the work of the contemporary spiritual

teacher Eckhart Tolle and his spiritual enlightenment.

This counter argument will help you move to the next level, which is an inner peace, a feeling of joy, comfort with patience and gentleness, and a new form of self-control. It's all wrapped up in two words I have added to his title, *The Power Of Now Is Love.*

The mechanics of this book are very simple. I've gone through chapter by chapter of Eckhart Tolle's book and presented counter arguments. Whenever I have referenced his material, you will find it in italics. My arguments generally take his material, provide some comment, present the source of his ideas, and expand his ideas, giving you a more complete understanding.

In my counter argument I will be referring to "Scripture"—as passages taken from the Bible. I will be using the terms "Scripture" and "the Bible" interchangeably. Unless otherwise indicated, all scriptural quotations are taken from the Holy Bible, New International Version.

THE TRUTH THAT IS WITHIN YOU

Eckhart Tolle writes, *I cannot tell you any spiritual truth that deep within you don't know already.*[3] I smiled at this statement, because in reality, this portion of his message is correct. Inside you dwells an inner voice that will teach you all truth. Eckhart Tolle, whether he knows it or not, is speaking about the Gift from the Father, known as the Spirit of Truth.

> [17] the Spirit of truth. The world cannot accept him, because it neither sees him nor knows him. But you know him, for he lives with you and will be in you.
> John 14: 17

Eckhart Tolle goes on to say that you will have *a profound transformation of human consciousness,* that you will no longer be enslaved and that you will enter into an *enlightened state.*[4] What might he be talking about when he talks about a *profound transformation* or an *enlightened state*? It sounds to me very much like this message:

> ² Do not conform to the pattern of this world, but be transformed by the renewing of your mind...
> Romans 12: 2
> *(Partial text)*

Transformed in Scripture is a metanoia. The Greek word metanoia has at its core a call to 'change one's mind' or undergo a deep transformation in perspective and way of life. Eckhart Tolle did not dream up these ideas; these ideas are not new to this age.

Eckhart Tolle goes on to devalue ancient religions, saying that they are *overlaid with extraneous matter that their spiritual essence has become almost completely obscured by it.*[5] In his words, one can see the sadness and hopelessness the world promotes, but in reality, there is life in the original teachings.

In reality, Eckhart Tolle has left out part of the message from Scripture. The verse from Romans chapter 12 begins with transformation but ends with a deeper understanding.

> ² Do not conform to the pattern of this world, but be transformed by the renewing of your mind. Then you will be able to test and approve what God's will is—his good, pleasing and perfect will.
> Romans 12: 2

When you read the full text, you note that there is a condition to the transformation of the mind: compliance. Compliance protects you, giving you discernment to know God's will; thereby, you are not conformed to the pattern of the world. The condition is that you are tuned to God's good, pleasing, and perfect will—tuned to Love. God is Love.

CHAPTER ONE
YOU ARE NOT YOUR MIND

THE GREATEST OBSTACLE TO ENLIGHTENMENT

Like Eckhart Tolle's material, this book points to a mystery within you: an inner power, an inner strength, a built-in wonder that was placed in you at conception. Eckhart Tolle would say, *Being is not only beyond but also deep within every form as its innermost invisible and indestructible essence.*[1] I know this innermost essence as the Rivers of Living Water, a power that resides within your gut.

Eckhart Tolle says *the word of God has become empty of meaning through thousands of years of misuse.*[2] In reality, there is a deep meaning that has not been lost—Love has not failed you!

Eckhart Tolle is close to the truth; there is a power within—the Rivers of Living Water. These rivers are placed there by the Gift of transforming Love.

(Learn about the Rivers of Living Water by reading Appendix A.)

This LOVE has endless possibilities, only limited by you and I. You are to open to it, look for its life and energy, and step into its flow. Step into Heaven.

Eckhart Tolle would have you disregard God, the person, and the concept. He makes the concept and reality of God, a thing to be spurned. He, like most North Americans, lives in an existential ontological condition; one might call "anomie." They are unconnected; there is an emptiness, a void. Therefore, it is easy to disregard the reality.

He talks about brokenness, suffering, the conflict in the world, and how your thoughts enslave. He writes that in this atmosphere *your mind creates an opaque screen of concepts, labels, images, words, judgments, and definitions that blocks all true relationship.*[3]

What relationship might this be, this *true relationship*? Could it be a relationship with LOVE?

When you read these kinds of comments, like *your mind creates an opaque screen*, you inculcate an emptiness inside. The void causes you to run from structured churches, from organized religion, and from tradition.

The reality is, however, that there is truth in these places. Man, from all eternity, has looked for fulfillment by joining community and walking together in these forms.

Eckhart Tolle is playing with 'anomie,' that feeling of emptiness, loss, worthlessness, hopelessness, helplessness, and existential pain. He calls himself *a contemporary spiritual teacher, who is not aligned with any particular religion or tradition.*[4] It's easy to bash those structures, bastions of hope that have supported and encouraged people for years.

I think the man, Eckhart Tolle, found some great and wonderful principles and took the opportunity to pass them on to the Now Generation. I am sure he was serious! The New Age movement was looking for his ideas, hungry for his thoughts, having rejected traditions. His message was received, and he is purported to be worth $80,000,000.00.

Do you want to find out about your true nature? Are you a genetic anomaly? Are you the product of an evolutionary accident, an evolutionary mutation that somehow worked out? Survival of the fittest! Is it confusing to consider these possibilities?

Was there some higher mover, prime mover, who set things into play with system and purpose and design?

Could the fact that each of you has his or her own unique fingerprint, his or her own DNA string, and his or her own iris biometric show a causal-relational dynamic that points to creation and a creator?

To see more of the causal-relational dynamic, you might look at Dr. Masaru Emoto's experiments, showing that water has memory; that when your words go out, they cause beauty or the lack of beauty and symmetry to be formed.[5] You affect the world around you.

Are you separate, or are you connected? Probably this is the most existential of ideas, causing Eckhart Tolle the most problems in *The Power of Now.* Are truth and reality mere constructed fictions? Are they merely ontological arguments?

Metaphysics, the branch of philosophy that deals with the first principles of things, including abstract concepts such as Being, knowing, substance, cause, identity, time, and space, deals with the nature of Being. Does *The Power of Now* affirm or imply anything about existence? I find that Eckhart

Tolle is presenting an interesting message in *The Power of Now*, but he fails to give you the answers to the above questions. I will attempt to develop his ideas and fill in the details. It is complex and probably cannot be done in one book.

You see, all of nature, all of these things you are finding in science, point to a unique and wonderful creative force: the Source of Love. Only Love could make you a unique human Being. Only Love could design the rhythm, the frequency, that all creation enjoys. When you are in harmony, the frequency produces beauty, cohesiveness, and awe, expressed in emotions like joy, peace, and contentment.

Your nature drives you to fill that void when you experience dissonance. Dissonance causes fracture, depression, confusion, and the like. These are obvious breaks with Love.

You and all humanity, are connected in this rhythm. I remember the term from existential philosophy, 'apart-ed-ness.' You are 'apart from,' yet at the same moment you are 'apart of.' This is your condition; you are a part of and a part from.

The world is not this clockwork thing; people are not machines. The world is more like an organism, a highly integrated, interconnected, organic thing, which extends through space and time. In that kind of environment, the way you think and the way you behave affect the outcome.

> [21] The tongue has the power of life and death, and those who love it will eat its fruit.
> Proverbs 18: 21

There is power. Creative power is emitted, produced and discharged, in a simple word or a simple intention of your mind. This power is the power of life and death. Eckhart Tolle called this *The Power of Now*.

You affect the reality that you see. Everyone is part of this organism.

Can you go backward and forward in time? Can you affect the world you live in?

The answer is yes! I constantly wake up in the morning and plan and create my day. I set the parameters and call down the blessings and guidance; come, Spirit of Wisdom, Spirit of Knowledge, Fortitude, and Peace. Try praying that prayer or maybe the Prayer of Abandonment, which I pray quite often.

PRAYER OF ABANDONMENT

Father,

I abandon myself into your hands;
do with me what you will.
Whatever you may do, I thank you:
I am ready for all, I accept all.
Let only your will be done in me,
and in all your creatures -
I wish no more than this, O Lord

Into your hands I commend my soul;
I offer it to you with all the love
                          of my heart,
for I love you Lord,
and so need to give myself,
to surrender myself into your hands,
without reserve,
and with boundless confidence,
for you are my father.

    —Brother Charles of Jesus

The day is set in motion. You are the musician, listening and attentive to the Spirit. Simply, your intention has an effect on the world. You do not control the world, but you surely have an effect on the outcomes. Practiced the presence of Love. Be attentive to Love!

The fundamental truth of unity is that you and I are one. Entanglement—you are one with each other, and you are one with Love.

In counselling, the word entanglement is described in these words:

> Entanglement happens when the boundaries in a relationship are blurred, and the emotional well-being of one or both participants is dependent upon the other in a way that sacrifices psychological health and autonomy.[6]

In physics the word entanglement is described in these words:

> Quantum entanglement is the phenomenon of a group of particles being generated, interacting, or sharing spatial proximity in such a way that the quantum state of each particle of the group cannot be described independently of the state of the others, including when the particles are separated by a large distance.[7]

As you practice, focus, and tune, you become an emergent property—in the same way that ballet or tango emerges from individual dancers, entanglement arises from the connection between particles.

Now, you do realize that the world is always bombarding you with stimuli and that you receive those stimuli and are receptive. The question that comes to mind is, are you just responsive, or are you a co-creator? If you are only responsive, then it is like a pinball being hit by the other balls, but that is not true. You are to seed in specifics into your world. You are to lay out the design. The old adage, 'good fortune is the residue of design,' comes into play. Your thoughts, your planning, and your practice affect the outcome, and longitudinally, you receive the benefits of your design. Your connection to Love produces fruit.

Can you imagine if everyone was sharing the same base of consciousness, Love? Could you imagine if Love drove all human behavior? Could you imagine that you were harmonious, fluid, rhythmic, and synced with those around you? Could you imagine if all your vibrations, your frequencies, had resonance with others? The fruit of this harmony and resonance would be: Love, Joy,

Peace, Patience, Gentleness and Self-Control.

God is Love. You cannot shrink from this statement of Scripture found in 1 John 4.

> [16] And so we know and rely on the love God has for us. God is love. Whoever lives in love lives in God, and God in them.
> 1 John 4: 16

In this relationship with Love, there is an inter-activeness. God is the origin of love, and through Him, love is revealed and experienced.

FREEING YOURSELF FROM YOUR MIND

Eckhart Tolle, what do you mean by *freeing yourself from your mind*? [8] He talks about *watching the thinker*.[9] You hear voices in your head. You are a bit mad and incessantly talking or muttering to yourself. Those voices, talking and muttering, are normal, he says. He concludes that you have to become impartial, and your thoughts are not who you are.

Scripture would state it differently: take every thought captive to Christ.[10]

You see, the mind is a battlefield, and you tend to be controlled by it until you realize that it is just a field of thoughts, comments, speculations, judgements, comparisons, vibrations, and frequencies—an energy field that gives and takes from your life. You tend to think that all the thoughts running through your mind are your own, when in reality, thoughts can come from four different sources. Thoughts come from four sources.

- They can come from the world around you.
- They can come from within yourself and your experiences.
- They can come from God, who is Love.
- They can come from the evil one, the prince of the world.

It is necessary in controlling the mind, *watching the thinker* as Eckhart Tolle would say, to take every thought captive.

> [5] We demolish arguments and every pretension that sets itself up against the knowledge of God, and we take captive every thought to make it obedient to Christ.
> 2 Corinthians 10: 5

Scripture says you are to take every thought captive. Why? It is so that you can test every thought, to hold it up before Love and say, "Is this from you, Love?" "Is this from you, Lord?" You are only to follow the things that come from Love. You are to be led by Love.

It makes sense then when Eckhart Tolle writes, *One day you may catch yourself smiling at the voice in your head, as you would smile at the antics of a child. This means that you no longer take the content of your mind all that seriously, as your sense of self does not depend on it.*[11] What in essence he is saying is that you come to know these thoughts, feelings, and emotions, and in knowing, it helps you to control the effects. You become detached from them and become more attached to that inner essence. You become connected to the presence—to Love.

ENLIGHTENMENT:
RISING ABOVE THOUGHT

By being in the presence, by being in God's presence, by being one with Love, you are no longer simply bouncing around like a pinball, but you are experiencing the essence of the immediate situation. You are living in the present experience. You start paying attention to every moment; you start experiencing every situation: the scent of the soap, the movement of your hands, the feeling of water, and the wonder of sound.[12]

You begin to experience peace that passes all understanding.

> [7] And the peace of God, which transcends all understanding, will guard your hearts and your minds in Christ Jesus.
> Philippians 4: 7

Love experienced gives the residue of peace—peace which transcends all understanding. This peace guards your heart and your mind.

EMOTIONS: THE BODY'S REACTION TO YOUR MIND

Eckhart Tolle goes on to talk about emotions and *unconscious mental-emotional reactive patterns.*[13] You know that through thought, emotions are exhibited, and the emotions may trigger physical or psychological effects in your body. Emotions cause biochemical changes. These biological chemical changes are aspects of the emotions. Anger is an example of when *the body gets ready to fight.*[14] Of course, you are not always conscious of all of this stuff, but you need to pay attention and become aware. Eckhart Tolle says *you are not usually conscious of all your thought patterns*; therefore, by observing *your emotions, you can bring them into awareness.*[15]

It is good to be aware of how you react. It is good to realize that you have learned behavior. You need to know yourself and your experiences. You begin to learn about them by first identifying the negative. You hold up the negative to Love. You open it to Love, asking for its source. These are the five steps in the *Five Fold Cycle – Method of Healing Personal Hurts: Healing Life's Hurts,* my original book.[16]

In the *Five Fold Cycle,* you begin by catching a negative and presenting it to God, presenting it to Love. You invite Love into the negative. Then you ask for the help of God's Holy Spirit to understand how this negative got into your life. You look for the root, the source, the first experience of this negative. The Holy Spirit, in His wisdom, grants you a Word of Wisdom; through His Love He grants you a Word of Knowledge; and through His omniscience, He grants you the Gift of Discernment. The Holy Spirit nourishes you with an understanding of the origin of the negative, inviting healing.

I enjoy how Eckhart Tolle writes about Scripture yet avoids it or devalues it. He says that emotions literally mean disturbances,[17] and that love, joy, and peace are deep states of Being. Of course they are, because they are the fruit of the Holy Spirit found in Galatians.

> [22] But the fruit of the Spirit is love, joy, peace, forbearance, kindness, goodness, faithfulness, [23] gentleness and self-control. Against such things there is no law.
> Galatians 5: 22-23

The three, *love, joy, and peace, are deep states of Being* writes Eckhart Tolle, and *they arise from beyond the mind.*[18] Of course they do, because they come from the Creator—the Great I AM! (Exodus 3:14)

Emotions, on the other hand, being part of the dualistic mind, are subject to the law of opposites. This simply means that you cannot have good without bad.[19] Because of this duality, you need to access the spiritual powers offered by the Holy Spirit to provide clarity.

Some of you have learned to lean on Scripture. You take the negative to Jesus on the Cross, where it can be exchanged for the positive. Emotions, their experience in your early life, can then be identified and transformed by Love.

(Learn about the Exchange at the Cross by reading Appendix B.)

Love takes your guilt and your shame. Love is a call, a reminder of who you are, His beloved, His children. He says to you, "You are Love," "You are Loved," "You have always been loved"—unconditionally Loved. These words come as a wave washing over you, breaking down walls.

It is not a Love that you can earn. This is not a Love you deserve. It is not conditional or limited. This Love is infinite, unchanging, and utterly beyond comprehension.

> [9] But he said to me, "My grace is sufficient for you, for my power is made perfect in weakness." Therefore I will boast all the more gladly about my weaknesses, so that Christ's power may rest on me.
> 2 Corinthians 12: 9

You strive, trying to prove yourself, trying to be good enough, when all Love wants is for you to trust your openness, connection, and relationship, rather than isolation.

> [8] He has shown you, O mortal, what is good. And what does the LORD require of you? To act justly and to love mercy and to walk humbly with your God.
> Micah 6: 8

There is a deep longing in you to reach out to Love. As I have said in my previous work, there is a hole that only Love can fill; I called it a God-hole.[20] This longing for Love, is the truth you have been searching for all your life.

By now you are starting to see the difference between Eckhart Tolle's writing and my counter argument. Eckhart Tolle encourages you to look at yourself as 'Being,' the source and pinnacle of life, while through Scripture you realize that your significance comes in relationship with the Creator, the Father. Peace that passes all understanding comes through relationship with the Creator.

To give some understanding of the problems of the world, Eckhart Tolle explains that *humans have been in the grip of pain for eons, ever since they fell from the state of grace.*[21] This is known as the fall of Adam and Eve, found in Exodus 2 and 3. According to the Scriptural tradition, Adam and Eve in the Garden of Eden were able to 'walk and talk with God' because they were in a perfect, sinless state, allowing them to have a direct and intimate relationship with their Creator. 'Walk' is understood in a figurative sense. 'Walking and talking with God' signifies a close, personal relationship and fellowship with Love. Their sin separated them from God, and we have suffered from this separation.

In this chapter, Eckhart Tolle began by referring to your *'innermost invisible and indestructible essence,'* which Scripture refers to as Rivers of Living Water—the indwelling Holy Spirit. Eckhart Tolle taught about the problem with *'unconscious mental-emotional reactive patterns.'* Scripture encourages you to catch those patterns and take each negative and present it to God, present it to Love. You are encouraged to invite Love into the negative, and Light will transform the darkness. In the *Five Fold Cycle,* you are given a *Method of Healing Personal Hurt;* negatives are transformed to positives through the Cross. It is all about Love!

(Learn about the *Five Fold Cycle – Method of Healing Personal Hurt* by reading Appendix C.)

You have probably noticed a difference between where Eckhart Tolle is focusing you and where Scripture focuses you. Eckhart Tolle encourages you to find a power within, to separate from *the grip of pain.* Scripture focuses you toward interaction with Love.

Love loves you on your good days, and Love loves you on your bad days. Love is there when you feel it and when you don't feel it. Love loves you when you do the right things, and Love loves you when you do not do the right thing, because Love is not contingent on you, but on Him. Love is not based on who you are, but on who He is. God is Love. Love poured out on you is based on God's character—His essence.

CHAPTER TWO
CONSCIOUSNESS:
THE WAY OUT OF PAIN

CREATE NO PAIN IN THE PRESENT

Eckhart Tolle implies that all pain in your life has two sources: *the pain that you create now, and the pain from the past that still lives on in your mind and body.*[1] He goes on to say, *That the greater part of human pain is unnecessary. It is self-created as long as the unobserved mind runs your life.*[2]

Further, Eckhart Tolle says that the pain from the past is the unconscious area of your life, where you don't want things to happen the way they happened, where there's resistance. He explains that the mind wants to remain in control, covering over the past and the future: *The mind always seeks to deny the Now and to escape from it.*[3]

It's all glorious, wonderful speculation! The reality is that you live out of the past into the present, that in the present moment you are to be one with your Creator. In this unique relationship, you can heal past trauma, and you can look forward to the future. In this relationship with Love, you are not driven by your unconscious, there is no denial or need to escape. Again, you will note that there is a bit of a contrast between Eckhart Tolle's approach and Scripture.

Scripture would direct you to accept these things in a relationship with Love's healing and lead.

Eckhart Tolle would call you to accept what was and make it your friend. He would call you to look at the past pains and their effects on your body and make them your friend. His idea of saying yes to the present moment and living in the moment, when understood through Scripture, is a good and healthy idea. *Surrendering to what is. Saying "yes" to life— and see how life suddenly starts working for you rather than against you.*[4] Most people in the helping field would agree with this principle: if you are positive and look positively towards the world, then things work out better.

A relationship with Love and working under Love's guidance would confirm these statements: *Always work with it, not against it. Make it your friend and ally, not your enemy. This will miraculously transform your whole life.*[5]

PAST PAIN: DISSOLVING THE PAIN-BODY

Eckhart Tolle states, *As long as you are unable to access the power of the Now, every emotional pain that you experience leaves behind a residue of pain that lives on in you. It merges with the pain from the past, which was already there, and becomes lodged in your mind and body.*[6] This portion of his message is correct; the pain accumulates. The negative energy is dumped on the body.

Obviously, you need to constantly be on your guard, bringing everything to the light, not allowing negativity to enter into your Being.

> [8] For you were once darkness, but now you are light in the Lord. Live as children of light [9] (for the fruit of the light consists in all goodness, righteousness and truth) [10] and find out what pleases the Lord. [11] Have nothing to do with the fruitless deeds of darkness, but rather expose them. [12] It is shameful even to mention what the disobedient do in secret. [13] But everything exposed by the light becomes visible—and everything that is illuminated becomes a light. [14] This is why it is said:

> "Wake up, sleeper, rise from the dead, and Christ will shine on you."
> Ephesians 5: 8-14

This Scripture is referring to goodness and evil. The same principle applies to the negative energy resulting from trauma. There is a need to constantly focus on Love's transformation. When you do not immediately bring things to the light, then you face the possibility of the trauma negatively affecting you.

Eckhart Tolle compares it to thinking you knew the person and finding out suddenly that something was alien in your relationship. He compares it to *irritation, impatience, a somber mood, a desire to hurt, anger, rage, depression, a need to have some drama in your relationship, and so on.*[7] These are all things that would catch you and make you wonder about all things from the past that are running your life. Eckhart Tolle calls this the *pain-body.*[8]

He states, you are caught up in these things, you have these ancient experiences that drive you. You have memories, pictures in your mind, that are attached to emotions, that are drivers that motivate negatively. At this point, Eckhart Tolle refers to a section from Saint Paul in Ephesians.[9]

> [13] *Everything is showing up by being exposed to the light, and whatever is exposed to the light itself becomes light.*
> Ephesians 5: 13
> (Version not specified.)

Everything is showing up by being exposed to the light.[10] Isn't it funny that Eckhart Tolle would take you to Saint Paul, to God's Word, in Scripture? Isn't it God that you're looking for, God the source of light? Isn't God Love? When you bring everything to the light, light transforms, and pain is dissolved.

Eckhart Tolle is developing the term that he calls *pain-body*. He describes it as a flaw within you that needs the illumination of God and goes on to talk about how you need to deal with it: bring that feeling inside you to your attention, and know that it is *pain-body*. Accept it. In doing this, you don't think about it, you don't judge it, and you don't analyze it. In reality...

Do you notice I am using that phrase, 'in reality,' quite often? Often, I feel, Eckhart Tolle is not in touch with what is real. To bring Eckhart Tolle's writings into reality, I am translating his statements into very simple Scriptural principles.

In reality, what the title *Dissolving the Pain-Body* means is that you are bringing perfect Light, God's Light, the Creator's Light, into the situation. It is quite simple actually. Healing occurs as you refocus by bringing your *pain-body,* the hurts and memories from your past, to the light. All things of God are quite simple. God is Love.

Eckhart Tolle says this is *The Power of Now*, but in reality, this power is not about being in the Now; it is the power of free choice—the choice to join Love. You can choose to bring the negative to the light or keep it and let it play in your subconscious. You can enjoy the pain. *(I am being facetious.)*

This act of bringing your negative inner feelings, experiences, emotions, through the Spirit of God, to be healed and renewed by the One who is Love, is called redemption. *The Power of Now is Love!*

Over and over Eckhart Tolle brings you to Christian principles. He labels it as your power, *The Power of Now*. In reality, Eckhart Tolle is co-opting the thesis that belongs to Jesus and applying it in this new way, in this New Age, and people are swallowing it up. They are excited about Eckhart Tolle's *timeless* and *profound* spiritual enlightenment.[11]

Jesus' position, His thesis, is expressed in two places in Scripture, first in Isaiah 61 and then quoted in Luke 4.

> [17] and the scroll of the prophet Isaiah was handed to him. Unrolling it, he found the place where it is written: [18] "The Spirit of the Lord is on me, because he has anointed me to proclaim good news to the poor. He has sent me to proclaim freedom for the prisoners and recovery of sight for the blind, to set the oppressed free, [19] to proclaim the year of the Lord's favor."
> Luke 4: 17-19

The thesis used by Eckhart Tolle, through which he has gained notoriety, belongs to Jesus, the Anointed One, the Messiah, the Christ. The Anointed One is sent to proclaim freedom to the prisoners. You can think of those prisoners as those suffering from *pain-body*. Jesus will free the prisoner from *pain-body* and will recover the sight of the blind. He will open your eyes and let you see clearly, no longer blinded by the hurts and pains, freeing you from *pain-body*. And therefore, you, the oppressed, go free.

It is actually a simple message. You could have looked it up in any Bible. The key point is choosing to follow the directions of the Anointed One, Jesus. It is using your free choice, the power of choice; making His story your story, His thesis your thesis. It is feeding on Love.

There is a Cherokee story that describes this conundrum in which you find yourselves. It is often titled The Story of Two Wolves or Be Careful Which Wolf You Feed.

The Story Of Two Wolves

One evening an old Cherokee told his grandson about a battle that goes on inside people.

He said, "My son, the battle is between two "wolves" inside us all.

One is Evil. It is anger, envy, jealousy, sorrow, regret, greed, arrogance, self-pity, guilt, lies, resentment, inferiority, false pride, superiority, and ego.

The other is Good. It is joy, peace, love, hope, serenity, humility, kindness, truth, benevolence, empathy, generosity, faith and compassion."

The grandson thought about it for a minute and then asked his grandfather: "Which wolf wins?"

The old Cherokee simply replied, "The one you feed."

EGO IDENTIFICATION WITH THE PAIN-BODY

Eckhart Tolle points out that you have learned a simple principle: by being *the watcher of what happens inside you, you have at your disposal the most potent transformational tool.*[12] He neglects to tell you, however, that this tool is a God-given gift. With your free will, you can choose to open these hurts to the Creator, to Love. Love, whose nature is wholeness, pureness, perfection, happiness, joy, peace, and patience, would gladly heal you.

This is what the Lord told Israel and Moses as they approached the promised land. It applies to each of you:

> [26] *He said, "If you listen carefully to the* LORD *your God and do what is right in his eyes, if you pay attention to his commands and keep all his decrees, I will not bring on you any of the diseases I brought on the Egyptians, for I am the* LORD, *who heals you."*
> Exodus 15: 26

Once again, the principle is quite simple. Listen to the Lord, follow His directions, and He will heal.

You learn from Eckhart Tolle *that only you can do this. Nobody can do it for you.*[13] This is true. You, in free choice, need to open to the transformative light.

Eckhart Tolle points out a common human problem at this point, that you and others tend to hang onto the familiar. Even if you are unhappy, you tend to acquiesce, comply, and think about the things that you know. Of course, you can always keep the *pain-body* and keep the familiar. Eckhart Tolle explains that the key is bringing it to your attention, being present to it, and initiating the transformation.

He says that sometimes you can come along others who are in that state of presence and that they can help to accelerate things. I think Eckhart Tolle is suggesting that you come alongside him, Eckhart Tolle the *contemporary spiritual teacher, who is not aligned with any particular religion or tradition.*[14] In reality, you need to approach people who have learned to connect with Love and Love's Spirit—the Holy Spirit.

THE ORIGIN OF FEAR

Eckhart Tolle presents a question: *You mentioned fear as being a part of our basic underlying emotional pain. How does fear arise, and why is there so much of it in people's lives?* [15]

He explains that *the psychological condition of fear is divorced from any concrete and true immediate danger. It comes in many forms: unease, worry, anxiety, nervousness, tension, dread, phobia, and so on. This kind of psychological fear is always of something that might happen, not of something that is happening now.* [16] The point he is making is that you are in the present, but you are looking towards the future, and that creates an anxiety gap.

The question is, who is running you? Is it the mind, or is it your ego? *Fear seems to have many causes. Fear of loss, fear of failure, fear of being hurt, and so on, but ultimately all fear is the ego's fear of death, of annihilation.* [17] Eckhart Tolle suggests that you disidentify yourself from these things; this portion of his message is correct.

Eckhart Tolle suggests that you come to the light, which is a Scriptural principle; the source of light is Love. As you drop *the psychological condition of fear* and come to the light, these unconscious patterns quickly dissolve.

Eckhart Tolle states, *so anyone who is identified with their mind and, therefore, disconnected from their true power, their deeper self rooted in Being, will have fear as their constant companion.*[18] The reality, however, is that it is not about you, your power, or your deep Being, but rather your connection to Being, to Love—Love is the great I AM.

The phrase 'Love is the Great I AM,' isn't directly found in Scripture; the concept of God as Love and the significance of Love as the greatest of all things is, however, a recurring theme.

The Scripture from 1 John will give you a more complete exegesis of this idea. How does God's Love compare to the Love of the World? And how do you participate in that Love, so that there is no fear?

> [5] They are from the world and therefore speak from the viewpoint of the world, and the world listens to them. [6] We are from God, and whoever knows God listens to us; but whoever is not from God does not listen to us. This is how we recognize

> the Spirit of truth and the spirit of falsehood. ⁷ Dear friends, let us love one another, for love comes from God. Everyone who loves has been born of God and knows God. ⁸ Whoever does not love does not know God, because God is love. ⁹ This is how God showed his love among us: He sent his one and only Son into the world that we might live through him. ¹⁰ This is love: not that we loved God, but that he loved us and sent his Son as an atoning sacrifice for our sins.
> 1 John 4: 5-10

You are either connected to Love or Love is absent in your life. Connected means open, listening, and following. You can tell who is connected and who is not, who has the Spirit of truth and who has the spirit of falsehood. The key is acting in Love; loving your fellow man and loving Love who is God. Love is the necessary component of the intimate inter-active relationship. It was modeled by Jesus, the Son of God. Love drives out fear.

> [18] There is no fear in love. But perfect love drives out fear, because fear has to do with punishment. The one who fears is not made perfect in love.
> 1 John 4: 18

THE EGO'S SEARCH FOR WHOLENESS

Another aspect of the emotional pain that is an intrinsic part of the egoic mind is a deep-seated sense of lack or incompleteness, of not being whole.[19]

This concept has been discussed earlier, that what you are looking for is the source of Love. Love is the only fill for this emptiness. As you approach your Creator and come into relationship, this hole in your psyche is satiated. You feel complete.

David in Scripture pictured it in Psalm 42.

> *[1] As the deer pants for streams of water, so my soul pants for you, my God. [2] My soul thirsts for God, for the living God. When can I go and meet with God?*
> *Psalm 42: 1-2*

Like the deer that pants for streams of water, your soul pants for God, the living God, the God of Love, to quench your thirst.

Striving for things, money, possessions, success, power, and recognition does not make you complete. Eckhart Tolle's description of the ultimate fear, which is death, stated, *Death is stripping away of all that is not you.*[20] He has the idea pretty well down pat. If you can empty yourself of all of these things that you are tied to, all the things you are using to fill yourself, and open to the Creator, to Being itself, then at the doorstep of death you will feel no fear.

This chapter focused on consciousness and the reduction of pain. The Cherokee story of two wolves described the conundrum in which you find yourself. Which wolf do you feed? You were instructed to be on your guard, to bring everything to the light, to not allow negativity to enter into your Being; this is a constant process of transformation. Scripture fleshes this out, directing you to develop a relationship with Love, to be like a branch to the vine. You are not the center; Love is the center, and all things come through Love. When you are attached to Love, Love will drive out fear.

CHAPTER THREE
MOVING DEEPLY INTO THE NOW

DON'T SEEK YOURSELF IN THE MIND
Eckhart Tolle explains, *You have already understood the basic mechanics of the unconscious state: identification with the mind, which creates a false self, the ego, as a substitute for your true self rooted in Being. You become as a "branch cut off from the vine," as Jesus put it.*[1] *He goes on to say, the ego's needs are endless. It feels vulnerable and threatened and so lives in a state of fear and want.*[2] *And finally, he states, So once you recognize the root of unconsciousness is identification with the mind, which of course includes the emotions, you step out of it. You become present.*[3]

Don't seek yourself in your mind. Don't let the unconscious drive you. You are encouraged to watch the mind and the ego; to be separate from it, and therein you find wholeness. Once again Eckhart Tolle is showing you that being in yourself, the 'I,' is most important.

In Scripture Jesus' message is more complete, that you are to be attached to the vine, be 'part of,' in relationship with, and working as one.

It is interesting that Eckhart Tolle takes one little thought from a line in Scripture or one little phrase and makes it out as the full teaching, but you know this is not true exegesis.

Let's look at the complete teaching of Jesus that Eckhart Tolle has avoided:

> [4] Remain in me, as I also remain in you. No branch can bear fruit by itself; it must remain in the vine. Neither can you bear fruit unless you remain in me. [5] "I am the vine; you are the branches. If you remain in me and I in you, you will bear much fruit; apart from me you can do nothing. [6] If you do not remain in me, you are like a branch that is thrown away and withers; such branches are picked up, thrown into the fire and burned. [7] If you remain in me and my words remain in you, ask whatever you wish, and it will be done for you.
> John 15: 4-7

You can see already that Eckhart Tolle left out some key lines. Verse 4 says, *remain in me as I also remain in you.* It defines the unity, the oneness that is necessary. This Scripture implies relationship, being one with; that to bear much fruit it is necessary to be a branch attached to the vine. It means being attached to the 'I AM.'

Verse 5 clarifies the relationship. *I am the vine; you are the branches.* It becomes quite obvious that you are to be in a relationship with the Creator, who is the source and summit of life. You are able to do nothing without Love.

Verse 6 emphasizes how a branch withers and dies, when it is not attached to the vine. The vinegrower throws it into the fire to be burnt. The image is quite easy to understand. When you are not attached to the vine, it means you, the branch, die.

Verse 7 gives you a powerful message, that if you remain in Him, Love, and His words from Scripture remain in you, *ask whatever you wish, and it will be done for you.* Health, healing, and wholeness are available for the asking. *Remain in me, as I also remain in you*—you are to be in relationship with Love.

END THE DELUSION OF TIME

Most of Eckhart Tolle's messages revolve around the act of being present—in the Now. *Trapped in time: the compulsion to live almost exclusively through memory and anticipation. This creates an endless preoccupation with the past and future and an unwillingness to honor and acknowledge the present moment and allow it to be.*[4] Wonderful words by Eckhart Tolle, but what do they mean?

He wants you to divest yourself of time and be in the present. It sounds like a good idea. But I question whether looking to the past and future is really a problem at all. Yes, the past influences you, but it does not have to define you. And yes, you have hopes for the future. But these are just part of the human experience that allows you to be more present with, more attached to, and more intimate with Love.

God sees time in a unique manner; while you, His creature, understand time sequentially—the present slipping into the past—the future slips into the present. God views the eternal past, present, and future in a single, divine instant. All time is at once before Him.

> [4] *A thousand years in your sight are like a day that has just gone by, or like a watch in the night.*
> Psalm 90: 4

A thousand years is like a day or a watch in the night. God is not caught up in time. When you are connected to Love—God is Love, you open to the experience and are not caught up in time.

The final statements in that section make more sense when you realize you are this unique combination of past, with future hopes, living in the present. *The eternal present is a space within which your whole life unfolds, the one factor that remains constant. Life is now. There was never a time when your life was not now, nor will there ever be.*[5] You might ask, is time an illusion, or is it just your present situation defined by the Creator, defined by Love?

NOTHING EXISTS OUTSIDE THE NOW

Nothing exists outside of the present, the Now. That is the key message from Eckhart Tolle's book, *The Power of Now*. I keep referring you back to Scripture. Let me put this concept from Eckhart Tolle in Scriptural terms.

Scripture teaches that people should not worry about the future, because each day has its own challenges. It also suggests that people should trust God daily and focus on the present.

> [33] But seek first his kingdom and his righteousness, and all these things will be given to you as well. [34] Therefore do not worry about tomorrow, for tomorrow will worry about itself. Each day has enough trouble of its own.
> Matthew 6: 33-34

The complexity of the verse is missed in Eckhart Tolle's book. First you must seek the Kingdom of God, seek Love and His righteousness, then all things will be given to you. Meaning, if you want peace, if you want joy, if you want wholeness and fulfillment, healing and health, you need to seek first the Kingdom of God. In completing this thought, Scripture states, Therefore do not worry about tomorrow, the future. It would seem obvious that the same thing applies to the past: do not worry about the past. You are being directed very clearly to focus on the present, but to do this in a relationship with the One who is Love.

A similar Bible verse is found in Philippians:

> ⁶ Do not be anxious about anything, but in every situation, by prayer and petition, with thanksgiving, present your requests to God. ⁷ And the peace of God, which transcends all understanding, will guard your hearts and your minds in Christ Jesus.
> **Philippians 4: 6-7**

Do you want peace that transcends all understanding? Do you want to have your hearts guarded and your minds one with Being, to be one with Love? Do you not want to be in Love?

Seek first Love's Kingdom:

> ³³ But seek first his kingdom and his righteousness, and all these things will be given to you as well.
> **Matthew 6: 33**

Present your request to God, who is Love:

> ⁶ Do not be anxious about anything, but in every situation, by prayer and petition, with thanksgiving, present your requests to God.
> **Philippians 4: 6**

Ask whatever you wish, and it will be done for you:

> [7] If you remain in me and my words remain in you, ask whatever you wish, and it will be done for you.
> John 15: 7

You might develop these messages in this manner: what you do in this life is an echo of what will be in Heaven.

THE KEY TO THE SPIRITUAL DIMENSION

In life-threatening emergency situations, the shift in consciousness from time to presence sometimes happens naturally.[6] Eckhart Tolle explains that it is because of the *intense conscious presence.*[7] He explains that is why people engage in dangerous activity like car racing or mountain climbing and such. The intensely alive state frees you from time awareness. But you do not need to engage in the dangerous activity or place yourself in that life-threatening mind state to find that *Spiritual Dimension.*

Eckhart Tolle implies that two statements from Scripture are confirming the practice of being in the Now. The statements are "*Take no thought for the morrow; for the morrow shall take thought for the things of itself"* and *"Nobody who puts his hand to the plow and looks back is fit for the Kingdom of God."* [8] Is that correct exegesis of those two Scriptures?

The first passage is from the Sermon on the Mount in Matthew's Gospel (Matthew 6: 38). In the passage, Jesus is teaching his followers about living a life of faith and trust in God. It is not a reference to time.

The second passage from Luke 9: 62 teaches that a true follower of Jesus must commit fully to the task of discipleship, without hesitation or looking back at the past, and must have a single-minded focus on following Christ. Once again, it is not a reference to time.

In reality, Eckhart Tolle has taken portions of a message and colored them to try and make his point. He titled this section *The Key To The Spiritual Dimension*, the key actually is a relationship with Love.

The Scripture Isaiah 26 gives depth and understanding to this section and to the *Key*.

> [3] You will keep in perfect peace those whose minds are steadfast, because they trust in you. [4] Trust in the Lord

> forever, for the LORD, the Lord himself, is the Rock eternal.
> Isaiah 26: 3-4

Scripture is expressing a clear principle: God, who is Love, promises He will keep you in perfect peace, whose minds are steadfast. Trust in the Lord is the key to having a steadfast mind and receiving peace.

What is meant by a 'steadfast mind'? Steadfast means your mind is fixed on something; in this case, your mind is fixed on God, who is Love. Because you trust in Love, rather than on external factors or personal strength, and because you have faith and reliance in Him, you will receive perfect peace. Scripture emphasizes that this perfect peace is a result of faith—trust.

Trust comes from knowledge and experience with God, that ongoing connection of the branch to the vine. This trust brings you security, because your foundation is rock solid—you are attached to the Rock eternal.

TRUSTING AND UNDERSTANDING GOD FOR HEALING

To trust and understand God fully, you need to embrace these theological conclusions and make them part of your life:

- God's love for you is unconditional—you were born of God.
- He has sovereignty over all things—He is the King of Kings and Lord of Lords.
- He is a loving Father, who will never abandon you—He has adopted you.
- Grace and redemption are freely given from God—God is Love.
- The Holy Spirit's role is to transform you—you are to be Born Again.
- Christian community is healing.
- There is hope of restoration and future glory in Christ.

You begin the healing process by making these theological decisions, integrating these truths into your life, and choosing to trust that God is working within you to bring about your transformation.

In summary of Isaiah, there is a promise to you, a state of tranquility and security, a peace that transcends understanding any worldly circumstances, when your mind is *steadfast*. It is the result of having your thoughts and beliefs firmly rooted in God, who is Love.

Referring to the German mystic philosopher Meister Eckhart, Eckhart Tolle quoted:

> *"Time is what keeps the light from reaching us. There is no greater obstacle to God than time."* [9]

The German mystic believed that time represents a significant barrier to experiencing the divine, suggesting that to truly connect with God, one must transcend the limitations of time and earthly concerns. Is that true?

In his writing, Eckhart Tolle implies that your preoccupation with the past and future prevents you from fully being present in the moment, which is where a deep connection with the divine can be found. I enjoy how Eckhart Tolle continues to take portions of Christian principles and ideas and apply them to his New Age enlightenment.

There is some sense of truth in his statement. Christian mystics teach that stepping away from the business of life, in silence and inner contemplation, helps one reach the divine experience of Love. The physical world can limit your ability to transcend. The step that Eckhart Tolle misses, however, is *Trusting And Understanding God For Healing,* the title of this section.

ACCESSING THE POWER OF NOW

Job, in Scripture, describes what Eckhart Tolle is trying to teach in this section. Job is referred to as a person experiencing nature in a new way, in a timeless dimension, knowing *the sacredness and mystery of life.*[10]

In this Scripture, Job's friends are berating him for his faith, his steadfast faith. Job replies:

> [7] "But ask the animals, and they will teach you, or the birds in the sky, and they will tell you; [8] or speak to the earth, and it will teach you, or let the fish in the sea inform you. [9] Which of all these does not know that the hand of the LORD has done this? [10] In his hand is the life of every creature and the breath of all mankind.
> Job 12: 7-10

From these lines you get a clear message that there is a connection between each of you and creation. This connection comes through the Creator, who gives you dominion over the plants of the earth, the animals, and the fish of the sea.

Saint Francis is an example of a person who Eckhart Tolle might say is in the presence, in the Now, a mystic. Saint Francis is always pictured with animals, in nature, comfortable, and unafraid. Certainly, this man, this saint, did not interrupt the world round him. He was peaceful, observed its presence, and was what Eckhart Tolle would call the *silent watcher*.[11] Saint Francis exhibits Love.

Love does not interfere with or *impair your ability to use time—past or future—when you need to refer to it for practical matters. Nor does it impair your ability to use your mind. In fact, it enhances it.*[12]

LETTING GO OF PSYCHOLOGICAL TIME
Eckhart Tolle is teaching about putting time in order and not being run by time. Psychological time *is identification with the past and continuous compulsive projection into the future.*[13] Clock Time is ok, because you use it to predict *the future by means of patterns and laws—physical, mathematical,*

and so on—learned from the past and take appropriate action on the basis of our predictions.[14] *The enlightened person's main focus of attention is always the Now, but they are still peripherally aware of time. In other words, they continue to use clock time but are free of psychological time.*[15]

Scripture has many verses that confirm Eckhart Tolle's thoughts about time. Ecclesiastes presents the idea that there is a season and a time for everything and that change is inevitable. You will remember the most famous lines from Ecclesiastes, often used at weddings and funerals.

> [1] There is a time for everything, and a season for every activity under the heavens: [2] a time to be born and a time to die, a time to plant and a time to uproot, [3] a time to kill and a time to heal, a time to tear down and a time to build, [4] a time to weep and a time to laugh, a time to mourn and a time to dance, [5] a time to scatter stones and a time to gather them, a time to embrace and a time to refrain from embracing, [6] a time to search and a time to give up, a time to keep and a time to throw away, [7] a time to tear and a time to mend, a time to be silent and a time to speak, [8] a time to

> love and a time to hate, a time for war and a time for peace.
> Ecclesiastes 3: 1-8

There is a time for everything under the sun. The challenge is to use time well and not be caught up in time.

You will remember earlier that Eckhart Tolle referred to everything being exposed to the light. This quote was taken from Ephesians and is only part of the verses. You will remember the comment earlier about exegesis, where it's necessary to take the whole and not just parts to understand the thesis. Let's now see how this applies to using your time.

> [10] and find out what pleases the Lord. [11] Have nothing to do with the fruitless deeds of darkness, but rather expose them. [12] It is shameful even to mention what the disobedient do in secret. [13] But everything exposed by the light becomes visible—and everything that is illuminated becomes a light. [14] This is why it is said:
>
> "Wake up, sleeper, rise from the dead, and Christ will shine on you."
>
> [15] Be very careful, then, how you live —not as unwise but as wise,

[16] making the most of every opportunity, because the days are evil. [17] Therefore do not be foolish, but understand what the Lord's will is. [18] Do not get drunk on wine, which leads to debauchery. Instead, be filled with the Spirit, [19] speaking to one another with psalms, hymns, and songs from the Spirit. Sing and make music from your heart to the Lord, [20] always giving thanks to God the Father for everything, in the name of our Lord Jesus Christ.
Ephesians 5: 10-20

Use of time has to do with using time well, good deeds, and blessing rather than cursing. Using time has to do with listening to the Holy Spirit, who is the bond of Love, because the Holy Spirit connects the divine and human nature in Christ. Bringing things to the light means exposing them to God's will. Once again Scripture is teaching about relationship, being one with, being able to hear, and being able to respond to the light, all of which requires an infilling of the Holy Spirit.

Scripture states, be filled with the Spirit (Ephesians 5: 18), inviting the Holy Spirit to dwell within you, in your temple, which is your body.

> ¹⁷ But whoever is united with the Lord is one with him in spirit. ¹⁸ Flee from sexual immorality. All other sins a person commits are outside the body, but whoever sins sexually, sins against their own body. ¹⁹ Do you not know that your bodies are temples of the Holy Spirit, who is in you, whom you have received from God? You are not your own;
> 1 Corinthians 6: 17-19

You probably haven't heard this message from Scripture stating that your body is God's temple—Love's temple. This temple is the home for Love.

> ⁵ And hope does not put us to shame, because God's love has been poured out into our hearts through the Holy Spirit, who has been given to us.
> **Romans 5: 5**

God's Love is poured into your heart through hope in the Holy Spirit. When you ask for the Holy Spirit to fill your temple, you receive the indwelling of Love. This Love will drive everything. It will filter what you see, how you think, and how you react to what happens around you.

As you look at alternate Scriptures, you will see the importance of receiving the whole exegesis. These Scriptural messages encourage a relationship with Christ Jesus, hearing the message of truth, and receiving salvation.

> [13] And you also were included in Christ when you heard the message of truth, the gospel of your salvation. When you believed, you were marked in him with a seal, the promised Holy Spirit,
> Ephesians 1: 13

You are to be sealed with the promised Holy Spirit. You are to receive the fullness of Love, to be marked in Him with a seal, sealed with Christ. Being Sealed can take you back to the image of a branch attached to the vine, a flowing relationship.

NEGATIVITY AND SUFFERING HAVE THEIR ROOTS IN TIME

Eckhart Tolle wants you to understand that you are not your thoughts nor your feelings; you have a greater consciousness that, once you access it, frees you from the pain you have been experiencing.

All negativity is caused by an accumulation of psychological time and denial of the present. Unease, anxiety, tension, stress, worry—all forms of fear—are caused by too much future, and not enough presence. Guilt, regret, resentment, grievances, sadness, bitterness, and all forms of nonforgiveness are caused by too much past, and not enough presence, states Eckhart Tolle.[16] Once again, you are given this wisdom without an exegesis of its source.

> [6] For this reason I remind you to fan into flame the gift of God, which is in you through the laying on of my hands. [7] For the Spirit God gave us does not make us timid, but gives us power, love and self-discipline.
> 2 Timothy 1: 6-7

The source of this peace and presence is a gift from the Father, God the Father, which can be received through the laying on of hands. It does not make you weak, powerless, or timid. This gift that the Father gives you, the indwelling Holy Spirit, comes with power, love, and self-discipline. Time, the accumulation of time, is not the issue. Your openness to the gift is the issue. Negativity and suffering are relieved as you fan into flame the gift of God.

Is it not amazing when you see the whole picture? Eckhart Tolle's message is a little out of focus. Scripture takes you to the source of truth.

Eckhart Tolle writes, *And yet this is the liberated state to which all spiritual teachings point. It is the promise of salvation, not in an illusory future but right here and now.*[17] Yes, Eckhart Tolle, this *peace of God which transcends all understanding,* is available now. It is there for the asking.

FINDING THE LIFE UNDERNEATH YOUR LIFE SITUATION

Why am I doing this? Why am I rewriting Eckhart Tolle's book *The Power of Now*? Am I after the man? No. I don't even know the man. Is there something that's eating at me? Maybe. As I read through his book, and I've read it before, I came to the sense that all Eckhart Tolle is doing is borrowing portions of wonderful truths and spinning them. In spinning them, people get caught, because of the time and the age, that particular century. He is like a folk hero, and I say, "Good on him."

As I started to play with editing these things, a life of its own began. I started to see that he is spinning partial truth, and my job is to point people to the complete truth—the source of truth. I would be very happy if each and every one of you learned about Scripture and developed a relationship with Jesus and His Holy Spirit.

In my ministry, I've never really been searching for money or fame. I'll be very happy that in my wake, I can see that others have been touched, opened their hearts, and received Love. As Eckhart Tolle states, you find *the life underneath your life situation.*[18]

Find the 'narrow gate that leads to life.' It's called the Now. Narrow your life down to this moment. Your life situation may be full of problems—most life situations are—but find out if you have any problem at this moment.[19] Once again, take a look at Scripture, where Scripture refers to the narrow gate. The narrow gate is a metaphor in the Bible that appears in Matthew 7: 13-14 and Luke 13: 24. It describes the path to life as narrow and difficult, while the path to destruction is wide and easy.

The Narrow and Wide Gates:

> [13]*"Enter through the narrow gate. For wide is the gate and broad is the road that leads to destruction,*

> and many enter through it. ¹⁴ But small is the gate and narrow the road that leads to life, and only a few find it.
> Matthew 7: 13-14

Scripture is suggesting that focus is necessary, that you are to keep your affairs in the narrow path, which will lead to life. Clearly Eckhart Tolle has caught that part of the message. Deal with one thing at a time. Deal with the present. Keep focused.

The narrow gate is a metaphor for the path to life, which is difficult and requires sacrifice. Jesus commands his followers to take the narrow path instead of the easy road to destruction.

> ²⁴ "Make every effort to enter through the narrow door, because many, I tell you, will try to enter and will not be able to.
> Luke 13: 24

The narrow door is God's grace through faith. In faith you open to Love, you listen to His Spirit, and you respond. It is about relationship.

How do you access the narrow gate and find this path to life?

It is all about yielding to the Holy Spirit. You are to be possessed by the Holy Spirit! You are to walk in the Spirit, allowing the Spirit to guide your lives.

Dr. Charles Stanley[20] describes it this way:

> To walk in the Spirit is to live moment by moment in dependency upon Him, sensitive to His voice and in obedience to Him.

Dr. Stanley describes three key words:

Dependent, Sensitive and Obedient.

Others have used the word possessed by the Holy Spirit. 'Possessed' means 'yielding' to the Holy Spirit.

When you invite the Holy Spirit into your body, you yield your body to the Holy Spirit. Thus, your body becomes a 'temple' of the Holy Spirit.

> [19] *Do you not know that your bodies are temples of the Holy Spirit, who is in you, whom you have received from God? You are not your*

own; [20] you were bought at a price. Therefore honor God with your bodies.
1 Corinthians 6: 19-20

The Holy Spirit resides within you. Your body is then a temple for the Holy Spirit. You honor the Spirit and become more dependent on Him. You become sensitive to Him, listening for His direction. You are leaning in that direction with an open heart, obedient to His direction in your life.

What is directing your life? What is important?

Yielding is all about allowing the Spirit to direct and guide: Dependency, Sensitivity and Obedience.

ALL PROBLEMS ARE ILLUSIONS OF THE MIND

It feels as if a heavy burden has been lifted. A sense of lightness. I feel clear... But my problems are still there waiting for me, aren't they? [21] This is a question posed to Eckhart Tolle. He responds by saying that if you focus your attention on the Now, in the moment, it is impossible to have a problem. Rather, it becomes *a situation that needs to be dealt with or accepted.*[22]

Yes, it makes sense; if you take every moment and deal with it, you really don't have problems. *When you create a problem, you create pain*, Eckhart Tolle states.[23] It all has to do with your focus. If you do not hold on to issues, nothing builds up—no pain. Eckhart Tolle goes on to say, *You also no longer contaminate the beautiful Earth, your inner space, and the collective human psyche with the negativity of problem-making.*[24]

I don't really agree with Eckhart Tolle; it's a nice fantasy that the problems are not problems but some kind of other reality. When your electric bill comes, you need to pay it. When your child breaks their arm, it would be a good idea to pay attention and head to the hospital.

The issue has more to do with focus and being attentive to where you keep your eyes. You start by taking your position in relation with Love, uniting your heart and mind with Love. Next, you navigate difficulties in your own life, meditate on Scriptural promises, and remain focused. You are reminded of the three relational words: Dependency, Sensitivity and Obedience. You step away from discouragement.

Proverbs, from Scripture, instruct on how to guard your heart and find life and health.

> [20] My son, pay attention to what I say; turn your ear to my words. [21] Do not let them out of your sight, keep them within your heart; [22] for they are life to those who find them and health to one's whole body. [23] Above all else, guard your heart, for everything you do flows from it. [24] Keep your mouth free of perversity; keep corrupt talk far from your lips. [25] Let your eyes look straight ahead; fix your gaze directly before you. [26] Give careful thought to the paths for your feet and be steadfast in all your ways. [27] Do not turn to the right or the left; keep your foot from evil.
> Proverbs 4: 20-27

Eckhart Tolle gives you the essence of the message. He always does! But he refrains from giving you the whole exegesis. Pay attention to what I say. That sounds like the direction; pay attention to the Creator God, to His words. Pay attention to Love. Turn your ear to my words, hear them. Do not let them out of your sight, look for them, read them. Keep them in your heart, meditate and muse on them. Dependent, Sensitive and Obedient to the Holy Spirit.

And why would you do that? Why would you keep your attention, hearing, sight, and heart focused on His words? The answer is found in verse 22, *for they are life to those who find them and health to one's whole body.* When you follow the Holy Spirit's lead, when you are tuned like a branch to the vine, then you receive the nutrients: grace, and Love. Therefore, you are in the best place, connected to Being. Problems wash away!

A QUANTUM LEAP IN THE EVOLUTION OF CONSCIOUSNESS

Eckhart Tolle states, *What we are doing here is a part of a profound transformation that is taking place in the collective consciousness of the planet and beyond: the awakening of consciousness from the dream of matter, form, and separation. The ending of time. We are breaking mind patterns that have dominated human life for eons. Mind patterns that have created unimaginable suffering on a vast scale.*[25]

Yes, you have to move out of the evil of the world. Yes, you have to realize that what you do affects the world around you. Eckhart Tolle goes on to say, *however you look at it, it is a quantum leap in the evolution of consciousness, as well as our only chance of survival as a race.*[26] This portion of his message is good, but you need to be aware that there is an overall confusion because his foundational message lacks the clear connection to Love. You have to cooperate with Love, and in that cooperation form a collective consciousness.

THE JOY OF BEING
Eckhart Tolle suggests that you test time by this kind of question: *Is there joy, ease, and lightness in what I'm doing?*[27]

In reality, you find Eckhart Tolle is using some portion of the larger principle:

> [19] *Do not quench the Spirit.* [20] *Do not treat prophecies with contempt* [21] *but test them all; hold on to what is good,* [22] *reject every kind of evil.* [23] *May God himself, the God of peace, sanctify you through and through. May your whole spirit, soul and body be kept blameless at the coming of our Lord Jesus Christ.*
> 1 Thessalonians 5: 19-23

Thessalonians from Scripture states: test everything, interact with the Holy Spirit, the Spirit of truth, and hold fast to what is good. This verse encourages you to critically examine situations and ideas, reject evil, and hold onto what is morally and spiritually sound. Love's grace sanctifies you through and through. Your whole spirit, soul, and body become blessed by Love.

Eckhart Tolle goes on to say, *So do not be concerned with the fruit of your action—just give attention to the action itself. The fruit will come of its own accord. This is a powerful spiritual practice.*[28]

Statements like, *When your deeper sense of self is derived from Being, when you are free of "becoming" as a psychological need, neither your happiness nor your sense of self depends on the outcome, and so there is freedom from fear,*[29] make a lot of sense.

Eckhart Tolle summarizes these statements in this manner: *you don't demand the situations, conditions, places, or people should make you happy, and then suffer when they don't live up to your expectations. Everything is honored, but nothing matters. Forms are born and die, yet you are aware of the eternal underneath the forms. You know that "nothing real can be threatened."*[30]

I find that Eckhart Tolle presents partial truths. Partial truths, although they might sound good, are flawed. Scripture is necessary to give depth and complete understanding. In this chapter he wants you to 'move deeply into the Now.' Scripture explains that you move out of illusion, you gain a quantum leap, you are comfortable with time, and negativity wanes when you are attached to Love. Dependence, Sensitivity, and Obedience in your relationship with Love bring the joy of Being. Finding life underneath your life situation is connecting with the indwelling Holy Spirit. Love has designed your temple as its home. You are Loved. God is Love.

CHAPTER FOUR
MIND STRATEGIES FOR AVOIDING THE NOW

LOSS OF NOW: THE CORE DELUSION

I am excited to write about these concepts of avoidance, being presented by Eckhart Tolle, but the man does go on, and on. He wants you to look at conscious and non-conscious drives. In his very eloquent way, he makes it out that you can separate yourselves from these two facets and be in the Now and into Being.

ORDINARY UNCONSCIOUSNESS AND DEEP UNCONSCIOUSNESS

Eckhart Tolle will take you through ordinary unconsciousness and deep unconsciousness. *Ordinary consciousness means being identified with your thought processes and emotions, your reactions, desires, and aversions. It is most people's normal state. In that state, you are run by the egoic mind, and you are unaware of Being.*[1] He goes on to say that it is a state of *low level of unease, discontent, boredom, or nervousness—a kind of background static. You may not realize this because it is so much a part of "normal" living…*[2]

The unease of ordinary unconsciousness turns into the pain of deep consciousness—a state of more acute and more obvious suffering and unhappiness—when things "go wrong," when the ego is threatened or there is a major challenge, threat, or loss, real or imagined, in your life situation or conflict in a relationship.[3]

You could get lost in all of this loquacity; Eckhart Tolle does go on. He has a tendency to be verbose, using way too many words, and he practices garrulity, excessive chatter. In this book, I would like to take you to what is the underlying principle driving all of his script.

WHAT ARE THEY SEEKING
Eckhart Tolle writes, *They are always seeking something... They are always uneasy and restless.*[4] Next, he refers to the words of Jesus: *Can anxious thought add a single day to your life?*[5]

Positioning yourselves, establishing the position of consciousness, and being in the Now have to do with knowing who you are—your identity.

Knowing that you are Loved — The Beloved.

Take a look at these Scriptures and consider the fact that you are 'The Beloved.' (I have added the word Beloved to each Scripture.)

<u>Beloved, Your Love proceeds from God's Love</u>:

> [7] Dear friends, *[Beloved]*, let us love one another, for love comes from God. Everyone who loves has been born of God and knows God.
> **1 John 4: 7**

<u>Beloved, Receive and Share that Love</u>:

> [12] Therefore, as God's chosen people, *[Beloved]*, holy and dearly loved, clothe yourselves with compassion, kindness, humility, gentleness and patience.
> **Colossians 3: 12**

> [11] Dear friends, *[Beloved]*, since God so loved us, we also ought to love one another.
> **1 John 4: 11**

¹ Follow God's example, therefore, as dearly loved children (*Beloved*), ² and walk in the way of love, just as Christ loved us and gave himself up for us as a fragrant offering and sacrifice to God.
Ephesians 5: 1-2

Beloved, In Living Love You Receive Health:

² Dear friend, *(Beloved)*, I pray that you may enjoy good health and that all may go well with you, even as your soul is getting along well.
3 John 1: 2

Poetry for The Beloved:

¹⁶ My beloved is mine and I am his; he browses among the lilies. ¹⁷ Until the day breaks and the shadows flee, turn, my beloved, and be like a gazelle or like a young stag on the rugged hills.
Song of Songs 2: 16-17

The title, *What Are They Seeking*, might be better written as 'Whom' are they seeking. By now you have a sense that you are the

Beloved. You sit in Love's presence, being one with, not encumbered by the future nor the past: no longer seeking, your uneasiness and restlessness subside.

DISSOLVING ORDINARY UNCONSCIOUSNESS

Make it a habit to monitor your mental-emotional state through self-observation. "Am I at ease at this moment?"... "What's going on inside me at this moment?" [6] Wonderful questions presented by Eckhart Tolle.

Scripture contrasts his direction, saying monitor your mental-emotional state by taking every thought captive.

You are reminded that thoughts come from four sources.

- They can come from the world around you.
- They can come from within yourselves and your experiences.
- They can come from God, who is Love.
- Or they can come from the evil one, the prince of the world.

In controlling the mind, it is necessary to watch the thinker, as Eckhart Tolle would say. Scripture offers a more complete message, directing you to take every thought captive to Christ.

What does it mean to 'take every thought captive'?

> [1] By the humility and gentleness of Christ, I appeal to you—I, Paul, who am "timid" when face to face with you, but "bold" toward you when away! [2] I beg you that when I come I may not have to be as bold as I expect to be toward some people who think that we live by the standards of this world. [3] For though we live in the world, we do not wage war as the world does. [4] The weapons we fight with are not the weapons of the world. On the contrary, they have divine power to demolish strongholds. [5] We demolish arguments and every pretension that sets itself up against the knowledge of God, and we take captive every thought to make it obedient to Christ.
> 2 Corinthians 10: 1-5

Verses 1 and 2 conclude that although you live in the World, you are different from the World; you live by different standards. Verses

3 and 4 explain that, although you live in the World, you do not respond to the World or wage war, as do others. Your weapons are different; they have divine power to demolish strongholds. You are to take captive every thought to make it obedient to Christ. You are to take every thought to the light—which is Dependence, expose it to the Holy Spirit—which is Sensitivity, and follow the Holy Spirit's lead—which is Obedience.

Eckhart Tolle poses these questions: *Have a look inside yourself. What kind of thoughts is your mind producing? What do you feel? Direct your attention into your body. Is there any tension?* [7] These are good reflective ideas to help you center.

Because you are accessing the Divine Being, Love, you have divine power to demolish strongholds—fear, loneliness, confusion, and the like. You can access power from outside the world, the Rivers of Living Water, that you can use to respond to the world.

What is necessary is to take every thought captive to Christ. You hold it up before Him and say, "Is this from you, Lord"? "Is this from you, Love"? You are to follow only the things that come from Love. *With practice, your power of self-observation, of monitoring your inner state, will become sharpened.*[8]

The following are some examples of self-observation and monitoring presented by Eckhart Tolle.

FREEDOM FROM UNHAPPINESS
Do you resent doing what you're doing? It may be your job, or you may have agreed to do something and are doing it, but part of you resents and resists it. Are you carrying unspoken resentment towards a person close to you? Do you realize that the energy you thus animate is so harmful in its effects that you are in fact contaminating yourself as well as those around you? [9] Eckhart Tolle is referring to a simple rule that I have taught in workshops for years. 'Whatever you send out goes out.' If you send out positives, it blesses people. If you send out negatives, it hurts, confounds the world around you, and may destroy people. Your tongue can bless or curse.

As I said before, Eckhart Tolle gives you part of the truth. Here are scriptures that explain more fully:

> [21] The tongue has the power of life and death, and those who love it will eat its fruit.
> Proverbs 18: 21

Do you want to negatively influence the world around you, or do you want peace and harmony? The answer is simple. If you want peace and harmony—to Love and be Loved—you need to watch and control your tongue.

> [10] For, whoever would love life and see good days must keep their tongue from evil and their lips from deceitful speech.
> 1 Peter 3: 10

Keeping control of your tongue will give you *good days* and show to others that you *Love life*. To live in Love, to Love life, means keeping your tongue. Once again it implies that peace and harmony are available; it is a choice.

> [1] A gentle answer turns away wrath, but a harsh word stirs up anger.
> Proverbs 15: 1

The World reacts to your tongue; a positive tongue *turns away wrath*, and a harsh tongue *stirs up anger*. Isn't it true!

> ²⁹ Do not let any unwholesome talk come out of your mouths, but only what is helpful for building others up according to their needs, that it may benefit those who listen.
> **Ephesians 4: 29**

Your words affect others around you. Scripture would suggest that you are to use positive words, bless others, and that your job is to Love those around you. In Loving, you will be Loved.

> ¹⁴ Make every effort to live in peace with everyone and to be holy; without holiness no one will see the Lord. ¹⁵ See to it that no one falls short of the grace of God and that no bitter root grows up to cause trouble and defile many.
> **Hebrews 12: 14-15**

There are many Scriptures that develop this idea of Love and Love's effects. In Hebrews 12, you are instructed that without your effort to Love and be Love, you and others are robbed of the ability to be one with Love, God being Love. Your job is to ensure no root of bitterness takes hold—negative roots cause trouble and defile many. You are to live in peace with everyone—to be holy.

How can you drop negativity...[10] Don't let bitter roots enter your world. Be the source of Love. Love exudes Love.

Many patterns in ordinary unconsciousness, on the other hand, can simply be dropped once you know that you don't want them and don't need them anymore, once you realize that you have a choice, that you are not just a bundle of conditioned reflexes.[11] Eckhart Tolle would say this is *the Power of Now*, but in reality, it is the Power of Love in relationship with Love.

Eckhart Tolle has an epiphany experience, where he and the world are one. I would say that this is an experience of being one with Love. God is Love.

The Power of Now is Love. It's all about Love.

Did you really need to hear from Eckhart Tolle *that humans killed in excess of one hundred million fellow humans in the twentieth century alone?*[12] Are you deceived into thinking it all just goes away? No, there is a choice: to move out of pain and move into Love. This section should have been titled Love Offers *Freedom From Unhappiness*.

WHEREVER YOU ARE, BE THERE
TOTALLY

Another example of avoidance offered by Eckhart Tolle is to *catch yourself complaining.*[13] *To complain is always non-acceptance of what is. It invariably carries an unconscious negative charge. When you complain, you make yourself into a victim.*[14] He tells you that you are to take action to drop the negative. Good wisdom.

I comment periodically that Eckhart Tolle has good wisdom. Let me ramble a bit about wisdom.

There is a Jewish tradition about wisdom—the wise man and the foolish man. There is the way of the fool, and there is the way of the wise man. In Christian exegesis, this has to do with how you obey, how you follow Him—Jesus. Within Eckhart Tolle's material you lose this message, because Eckhart Tolle is saying it is in you, in the Now, and he leaves out the complexity that it is 'in relationship' that you find wisdom.

Some see Jesus as a prophet, others as a great teacher, a model of justice, or a holy man, but Saint Peter, also known as Simon Peter, explained the connection with God the Father.

> [13] When Jesus came to the region of Caesarea Philippi, he asked his disciples, "Who do people say the Son of Man is?" [14] They replied, "Some say John the Baptist; others say Elijah; and still others, Jeremiah or one of the prophets." [15] "But what about you?" he asked. "Who do you say I am?" [16] Simon Peter answered, "You are the Messiah, the Son of the living God."
> Matthew 16: 13-16

Mark 8: 27-30 repeats this story found in Matthew 16. Peter declares that Jesus is the Messiah, Son of the Living God. Peter's reference to *Son of the living God* was to contrast with the gods of clay and stone and even the Roman Emperor, who was thought of as a god. Jesus, the Son of God, was alive on earth and after His resurrection continues to be alive. The belief in Jesus' resurrection is central to Christianity, affirming that He overcame death and ascended to heaven and continues to be present, loving, interceding, and advocating for your needs and desires.

I have mentioned the word 'relationship' being important. As you read the following story, you might think deeply about the need for relationship and the need to be built on a strong foundation—a rock-solid foundation.

There is a story in Scripture about a foolish man and a wise man building a house. The house represents their world, their life. You might put yourself in the story as the builders.

The Wise and Foolish Builders

[24] "Therefore everyone who hears these words of mine and puts them into practice is like a wise man who built his house on the rock. [25] The rain came down, the streams rose, and the winds blew and beat against that house; yet it did not fall, because it had its foundation on the rock. [26] But everyone who hears these words of mine and does not put them into practice is like a foolish man who built his house on sand. [27] The rain came down, the streams rose, and the winds blew and beat against that house, and it fell with a great crash."

The Authority of Jesus

[28] When Jesus had finished saying these things, the crowds were amazed at his teaching, [29] because he taught as one who had authority, and not as their teachers of the law.
Matthew 7: 24-29

Are you the wise man building your house on a solid foundation, or are you foolishly building your home on the sand? Are you building on solid, rock-solid foundations? A deeper question might be, what is the foundation, or maybe it is better to say, who is your foundation? Is your foundation based on Love—in Love?

Here is a little phrase upon which you might muse. It is often found in discussions about the nature of God's love.

Love is not based on who you are, but who He is.

These are the kinds of things you need to realize: when you are looking at wisdom, its exegesis is necessary. Wisdom comes through the Spirit of God; wisdom comes through Love. There is a relationship, a relationship with the Creator, the foundation, the source and Being, the bedrock known as Love.

> [11] *Wisdom teaches her children and gives help to those who seek her.* [12] *Whoever loves her loves life, and those who seek her from early morning are filled with joy.* [13] *Whoever holds her fast inherits glory, and the Lord blesses the place she enters.* [14] *Those who serve her minister to the Holy One; the Lord loves those who love her.* [15] *Those who obey her will judge the nations, and all who listened to her will live secure.* [16] *If they remain faithful, they will inherit her; their descendants will also obtain her.*
> Sirach 4: 11-16 NRSV

On the bedrock of Love, you can begin to take action. You no longer need to be *stuck in an unhappy situation.*[15] *If you remain stuck, you learn nothing. Is fear preventing you from taking action? Acknowledge the fear, watch it, take your attention into it, be fully present with it. Doing so cuts the link between the fear and your thinking. Don't let fear rise up into your mind.*[16] Eckhart Tolle goes on to say that this is *The Power of Now*, but I suggest that this is the Power of Love. As you step in to Love, open your heart to Love, present the negative to Love, you become one with Love. Love drives out all fear.

> [18] There is no fear in love. But perfect love drives out fear, because fear has to do with punishment. The one who fears is not made perfect in love.
> 1 John 4: 18

The title of this section might better be written *Wherever You Are, Be There Totally* with Love at your side. Love drives out fear and does not let worry or anxiousness punish you. Fear is made perfect in Love.

Eckhart Tolle goes on to ask a number of questions: *is there something you "should" be doing but are not doing it?*[17] *Are you stressed?*[18] *Are you worried?*[19] *Are you a habitual "waiter"? How much of your life do you spend waiting?* [20] He explains that all of these are negatives under your control. All of these strategies, he says, are *denying the present moment and are part of the ordinary unconsciousness.*[21] This being true, you are told to monitor *your inner mental-emotional state.*[22] Follow his direction, but do it while standing on the solid ground that is Love.

You were made by Love and for Love. If you don't have that connection to Love, you don't have anything. God is Love. It doesn't say God has Love. It says God is Love; Love is His nature. Love is the essence of God; it's the nature of God to Love. God is Love.

You need to look at these things, meditate on them, and put them into practice.

THE INNER PURPOSE OF YOUR LIFE'S JOURNEY

I would like to review some of Eckhart Tolle's reasoning under this title. He says that your journey has an outer purpose and an inner purpose. *The outer purpose is to arrive at your goal or destination, to accomplish what you set out to do, to achieve this or that, which, of course, implies future.*[23] He warns that if the future becomes *more important to you than the step you are taking now, then you completely miss the journey's inner purpose...*[24] Eckhart Tolle explains that, *The outer purpose belongs to the horizontal dimension of space and time; the inner purpose concerns a deepening of your being in the vertical dimension of the timeless Now.*[25] All of that verbosity is supposed to impress you. Are you vertical, or are you horizontal? Are you now, or are you future? One could label Eckhart Tolle's writing as circumlocution: going round and round in a wordy way without ever getting to the heart of the matter.

Then he goes on to talk about the *light of Being. This one step then becomes transformed into an expression of perfection, an act of great beauty and quality. It will have taken you into Being, and the light of Being will shine through it.*[26] Very impressive language and wonderful images, but based on what?

At this point of Eckhart Tolle's writing, I think you have to start looking inside—try to find focus. What is this *light of Being*? What is inside you that has to shine forth? Let me take you to the source of this teaching. It has to do with the power inside. It has to do with the gift of the Father that I spoke about earlier.

ACCESSING THE RIVERS OF LIVING WATERS

> [37] On the last and greatest day of the festival, Jesus stood and said in a loud voice, "Let anyone who is thirsty come to me and drink. [38] Whoever believes in me, as Scripture has said, rivers of living water will flow from within them." [39] By this he meant the Spirit, whom those who believed in him were later to receive. Up to that time the Spirit had not been given, since Jesus had not yet been glorified.
> John 7: 37-39

From John 7 you come to understand that there is depth to this teaching regarding light from within. Jesus refers to it as Rivers of Living Water.

In the Old Testament stories, the Holy Spirit was only seen on or emanating from significant figures, such as the prophets, Moses, and King David. In John's Gospel from the New Testament, Jesus explains that when He is glorified, the Father will send His Spirit, the Holy Spirit. The Holy Spirit is the 'gift' from God the Father. Then, and only then, will you be able to access the Rivers of Living Waters. These rivers will flow from within you, from within your body, the Temple of God.

Eckhart Tolle gives you a hint of this teaching. Let's go on to learn more.

Did you notice that Scripture refers to accessing the 'Rivers,' not one river, but many Rivers of Living Waters? It is not a little gurgling stream or trickling brook. It is a river, and not just a river, but many rivers. In other words, there is an endless supply: Let anyone who is thirsty come to me and drink. All you have to do is believe, Whoever believes in me, as Scripture has said, rivers of living water will flow from within them. It is quite simple, as are all things of God, who is Love.

How are you going to get the Rivers of Living Water flowing from within? John's Scripture says, *Let anyone who is thirsty come to me and drink,* and that *living waters will flow from within them*—from their belly, from within. Drinking might be thought of as figurative: breathing might be clearer. You take a breath, inviting the Holy Spirit to fill you; you choose to let the Holy Spirit enter into your body, the Temple—your Being. Next you can release that Holy Spirit out to the world around you: your home, your work, and any environment in which you live. The outflow will bring Love into your world and will bring light into the world.

THE PAST CANNOT SURVIVE IN YOUR PRESENCE

Eckhart Tolle answers a question about investigating the unconscious past, memories, thoughts, emotions, desires, and reactions, explaining that *the challenges of the present will bring it out.*[27]

He claims that whatever you need to know about the past could be freed in the present, there's no need to go dredging up the past. He goes on to say that this is *The Power of*

Now. That is the key. None other than the power of your presence, your consciousness liberated from thought forms.[28] These are interesting thoughts, not right or wrong, but they are not complete. As you will see, the Scriptures that follow will flush them out.

Eckhart Tolle explains the process: *Give attention to the present; give attention to your behavior, to your reactions, moods, thoughts, emotions, fears, and desires as they occur in the present. There's the past in you... you are dealing with the past and dissolving it through the power of your presence.* [29]

Scripture develops this further in Philippians:

> [6] Do not be anxious about anything, but in every situation, by prayer and petition, with thanksgiving, present your requests to God. [7] And the peace of God, which transcends all understanding, will guard your hearts and your minds in Christ Jesus. [8] Finally, brothers and sisters, whatever is true, whatever is noble, whatever is right, whatever is pure, whatever is lovely, whatever is admirable—if anything is excellent or praiseworthy—think about such

things. ⁹ Whatever you have learned or received or heard from me, or seen in me—put it into practice. And the God of peace will be with you.
Philippians 4: 6-9

You can find more meaning to Eckhart Tolle's message by applying Philippians. You are not to be anxious about anything. To receive the peace that transcends all understanding, you refocus, petitioning Love with a thankful heart. You focus on whatever is pure, lovely, admirable, excellent, and praiseworthy. As you practice this refocusing, the past slips away, and healing occurs.

As you become more conscious of your present reality, you may suddenly get certain insights as to why your conditioning functions in those particular ways—for example, why your relationships follow certain patterns—and you may remember things that happened in the past or see them more clearly. [30]

With Philippians 4 in mind, you can see that Eckhart Tolle's ideas are approaching the scriptural process of healing. In reality the process is that you bring the past into the present, opening it to Love and Love transforms. As you keep your focus on positives, often you will come to understand the complexity of the old patterns of your life.

These old patterns change, and you move on—*the past cannot survive in your presence*[31]—in your experience of Love.

CHAPTER FIVE
THE STATE OF PRESENCE

IT'S NOT WHAT YOU THINK IT IS

Eckhart Tolle has you thinking about the presence, encouraging you to close your eyes and enter into Being. He goes on to say, *To stay present in everyday life, it helps to be deeply rooted within yourself; otherwise, the mind, which has incredible momentum, will drag you along like a wild river.*[1] I smile when I read this statement, because he is close to the truth and the fullness but misses the mark.

Listen to this Scripture found in Colossians 2:

> [2] *My goal is that they may be encouraged in heart and united in love, so that they may have the full riches of complete understanding, in order that they may know the mystery of God, namely, Christ,* [3] *in whom are hidden all the treasures of wisdom and knowledge.* [4] *I tell you this so that no one may deceive you by fine-sounding arguments.* [5] *For though I am absent from you in body, I am present with you in spirit and delight to see how*

disciplined you are and how firm your faith in Christ is.

Spiritual Fullness in Christ

⁶ So then, just as you received Christ Jesus as Lord, continue to live your lives in him, ⁷ rooted and built up in him, strengthened in the faith as you were taught, and overflowing with thankfulness.

⁸ See to it that no one takes you captive through hollow and deceptive philosophy, which depends on human tradition and the elemental spiritual forces of this world rather than on Christ.

⁹ For in Christ all the fullness of the Deity lives in bodily form, ¹⁰ and in Christ you have been brought to fullness. He is the head over every power and authority.

Colossians 2: 2-10

The Scripture warns you about being deceived by fine-sounding arguments. Finding peace in the present is not about closing your eyes and Being. Finding peace in the present is about being one with Love, rooted and built up in Him, strengthened in the faith, and overflowing with thankfulness. You are to enter into the Rivers of Living Water, flowing with them as the currents' flow guides you. You gain spiritual fullness, the riches of complete *understanding,* when you are attached to Love, for in Love lies *the fullness of the Deity.*

THE ESOTERIC MEANING OF 'WAITING'

Eckhart Tolle explains, *In a sense, the state of presence could be compared to waiting. Jesus used the analogy of waiting in some of his parables.*[2]

He says this is not a bored or restless kind of waiting. *There is a quantitatively different kind of waiting, one that requires your total alertness… This is the kind of waiting Jesus talks about. In that state, all your attention is in the Now.*[3] Interesting that Eckhart Tolle would refer you once again to Jesus!

Let's look at the Scriptures:

> [14] Wait for the Lord; be strong and take heart and wait for the Lord.
> Psalm 27: 14

Simply you are told to take heart, be strong, and wait for the Lord—wait for Love. The Scripture implies security and trust.

> [28] Do you not know? Have you not heard? The LORD is the everlasting God, the Creator of the ends of the earth. He will not grow

> tired or weary, and his understanding no one can fathom. ²⁹ He gives strength to the weary and increases the power of the weak. ³⁰ Even youths grow tired and weary, and young men stumble and fall; ³¹ but those who hope in the LORD will renew their strength. They will soar on wings like eagles; they will run and not grow weary, they will walk and not be faint.
> Isaiah 40: 28-31

Once again Scripture is pointing you to Love, the Lord, the Creator, assuring that in Him you receive strength and power to soar like the eagles. Even when you are tired and weary, stumble and fall, Love will carry you. Wait, attend to Love, who will provide for you.

> ²² Because of the LORD's great love we are not consumed, for his compassions never fail. ²³ They are new every morning; great is your faithfulness. ²⁴ I say to myself, "The LORD is my portion; therefore I will wait for him." ²⁵ The LORD is good to those whose hope is in him, to the one who seeks him; ²⁶ it is good to wait quietly for the salvation of the LORD.
> Lamentations 3: 22-26

Love never fails. Love's provisions are new every morning. You are to wait on Love, who will bring 'salvation.'

It is good to wait quietly for the salvation of the LORD. Salvation is the central theme in Scripture, the deliverance of the people through faith. Salvation often refers to deliverance from physical danger, oppression, and the fear of death. In this close relationship with Love, a branch to the vine, you experience a peace and security; waiting is not a trial.

> [1] Truly my soul finds rest in God; my salvation comes from him. [2] Truly he is my rock and my salvation; he is my fortress, I will never be shaken.
>
> [5] Yes, my soul, find rest in God; my hope comes from him. [6] Truly he is my rock and my salvation; he is my fortress, I will not be shaken. [7] My salvation and my honor depend on God; he is my mighty rock, my refuge. [8] Trust in him at all times, you people; pour out your hearts to him, for God is our refuge.
> **Psalm 62: 1-2; 5-8**

In trusting, resting, being rock solid, and being comfortable, you have identity; all are provisions of Love.

In reality, Eckhart Tolle has not presented the full message about waiting. Jesus is teaching his followers that waiting means actively hoping in, trusting in, and anticipating Love's timing and plan. You are to practice it with a patient attitude, submitting to Love's will, even when answers or desired outcomes are not immediately apparent. It is not passive inactivity but a stance of faith and reliance on Love's goodness and sovereignty.

BEAUTY ARISES IN THE STILLNESS OF YOUR PRESENCE

Eckhart Tolle calls it *satori*—presence, that *flash of insight, a moment of a no-mind and total presence.*[4] The Christian mystics, who enter into Love call it transcendence. This phenomenon is not a new experience to the mystics, and it is available to you.

Presence is needed to become aware of the beauty, the majesty, the sacredness of nature. Have you ever gazed up into the infinity of space on a clear night, awestruck by the absolute stillness and inconceivable vastness of it all? Have you listened, truly listened, to the sound of a mountain stream in the forest? Or to the song of a blackbird at dusk on a quiet summer evening? ⁵ These are the things that Eckhart Tolle compares to transcendence—satori. It is that spiritual awe that inspires. It gives life meaning. In traditional forms of belief, one might call it spiritual transcendence. It is core to your Being, that spiritual nature that enables you to transcend any experience at hand and seek meaning and purpose, to have faith, to love, to forgive, to pray, to meditate, to worship, and to see beyond the physical here and now.

Spiritual transcendence is that inner force that animates your human life. You breathe in the Holy Spirit, the divine, the Spirit who influences or acts upon you, opening you to hearing, receiving, and responding to sacred revelation. You are opening to Love, the supreme or ultimate reality, the being perfect in power, wisdom, and goodness, who is worshipped as Creator and Ruler of the universe.

Eckhart Tolle says, *Could it be that this nameless essence and your presence are one and the same?* ⁶ What he does not understand is that the Spirit of Love is inside you. You are not the Spirit of Love. Love is a gift you can participate in. Love has been within you, before you were born, as it says in Jeremiah.

> [5] "Before I formed you in the womb I knew[a] you, before you were born I set you apart; I appointed you as a prophet to the nations."
> Jeremiah 1: 5
> Footnotes
> [a] Or *chose*

Love knew you before your creation, formed you in your mother's womb, and set you apart as a unique individual. There will be no other like you. Love has appointed you, chosen you.

The keys of spiritual transcendence are to find the wonder of stillness and to meditate and contemplate. In doing so, you empty yourself, settle into the Now and enter into spiritual transcendence. There is a renewed sense of enthusiasm, hope, and inner strength. Spiritual transcendence can help you face your physical differences and challenges with a clearer perspective, rising above the limits and pain.

You are tuning yourself into oneness with Love. You will notice that what is inside you is different than what is outside of you—'apart of and apart from.'

You will remember Romans 12:

> ²Do not conform to the pattern of this world, but be transformed by the renewing of your mind. Then you will be able to test and approve what God's will is—his good, pleasing and perfect will.
> Romans 12: 2

Spiritual transcendence is an essential quality of Love, Love's Being and character. Love is beyond the material, the natural. Love might be called supernatural, not to be molded or conformed to this world.

Spiritual transcendence is experiencing Love in your spirit. Spiritual transcendence often comes in small doses, giving you a taste of Heaven.

REALIZING PURE CONSCIOUSNESS

Erkhart Tolle gives you a complex idea that he has formed. He articulates it, giving it multiple levels and mysterious understandings. Yet, do these ideas really hold water?

Realizing Pure Consciousness—When you become conscious of Being, what is really happening is that Being becomes conscious of itself. When Being becomes conscious of itself—that's presence. Since Being, consciousness, and life are synonymous, we could say that presence means consciousness becoming conscious of itself, or life attaining self-consciousness. But don't get attached to the words, and don't make an effort to understand this.[7]

Eckhart Tolle, the man, has the mental capacity to play with things and make them sound mysterious, important, transcendent, and necessary for one to be fulfilled. He wants you to be the center of life, but you are not. You are a creation, a special and unique creation—'Chosen.' You are important in relationship to Love—'Beloved.'

The reality comes to bear when you read the next section. Eckhart Tolle explains that *in the Bible, God declares, I am the Alpha and the Omega, and I am the living One."*[8] In that statement, surprisingly, he gives you the timeless truth that you are not the center of life. First, there is the Creator, who is timeless, omnipotent, omniscient, and omnipresent. God, who is Love, is *the essence of everything that ever has been and ever will be…*[9]

Eckhart Tolle would want you to agree with this statement: *In present-day humans, consciousness is completely identified with its disguise. It only knows itself as form and therefore lives in fear of the annihilation of its physical or psychological form. This is the egoic mind, and this is where considerable dysfunction sets in. It now looks as if something had gone very wrong somewhere along the line of evolution.*[10] Eckhart Tolle tends to make statements like this, causing confusion, making it seem like he knows and understands truth.

In reality, the truth is not *lila*,[11] the label Eckhart Tolle took from the East Indian idea that God is playing a divine game, but rather that Love has intentional interaction with you, His creation—the branch attached to the vine. In this divine interaction, Love takes you to new levels. There is enlightenment—states of heightened awareness, inner peace, and understanding of the interconnectedness of all life.

Scripture has these beautiful jewels that speak to this spiritual transcendence.

> [18] I pray that the eyes of your heart may be enlightened in order that you may know the hope to which he

> has called you, the riches of his glorious inheritance in his holy people,
> Ephesians 1: 18

Paul, an apostle of Christ Jesus, asks that the eyes of your heart may be enlightened. This phrase calls you to spiritual perception and understanding. The heart was considered the center of intellect and emotion, not just feelings. Enlightenment refers to divine illumination, sometimes called the eyes of your understanding.

I went looking for some depth to these ideas from Scripture and came across Ellicott's Scripture commentary.[12] It explains enlightenment in reference to the phrases eyes of your understanding or the eyes of your heart.

Ellicott's Scripture commentary explains:

> Ephesians 1: 18 —The eyes of your understanding—The true reading is *of your heart,* for which the words "of your understanding" have been substituted so as to yield a simpler and easier expression. The heart is similarly spoken of in relation to spiritual perception in Romans 1: 21;

1 Corinthians 2: 9; 1 Corinthians 4: 5; it signifies the inner man in his entirety, and the phrase here used seems to convey the all-important truth that for the knowledge of God, all the faculties of understanding, conscience, and affection must be called into energy by the gift of the light of God.

You are reminded once again about light, the light of God—Love. God is not playing a divine game, but rather Love has intentional interaction with you, His creation, His Beloved. There is an intelligent designer. The more you tune to Love, the more stillness and the more freedom you will have from what Eckhart Tolle calls *thought forms*.[13]

CHRIST: THE REALITY OF YOUR DIVINE PRESENCE

I am enjoying Eckhart Tolle's discussion of the 'I Am,' Christ, and God-essence. He says, *Don't get attached to any one word. You can substitute "Christ" for presence, if that is more meaningful to you. Christ is your God-essence or the self...*[14] I am saddened by this message.

It seems quite confusing because Eckhart Tolle presents a complicated message. What he presents is not the full picture. First, you must establish the meaning of 'Christ.' In the original Hebrew the word used for Christ was *'mashiyach.'* The Hebrew dictionary defines *'mashiyach'* as an 'anointed one' or 'Messiah.' Christ is the anointed one referred to in the Old Testament and is identified as Jesus the Christ in the New Testament.

There is more complexity. Jesus, the Christ, is the second person of the Blessed Trinity—Father, Son, and Holy Spirit. The Trinity is defined as three persons in one Godhead according to Christian exegesis. The Trinity is a mystery.

The Father has given you and I the gift of the indwelling Holy Spirit, that River of Living Water that flows from within. Presence is an intentional interaction with the indwelling Holy Spirit. The Holy Spirit connects you with the Father and the Son—the I Am.

In this relationship you enter into presence.

There is a danger in Eckhart Tolle's ideation. He has stepped into a theoretical flaw.

The nightmare became unbearable and that triggered the separation of consciousness from its identification with form. I woke up and suddenly realized myself as the I Am and that was deeply peaceful.[15]

In his description of his awakening, he says, *'I woke up and suddenly realized myself as the I Am.'* Now you can't argue with the man, but one could suggest that his conclusion was flawed. What if he should have concluded by saying, "One with I Am"? Or what if he said, "Being one with presence—apart of, yet apart from"?

'The reality of your divine presence' is that you are connected with Love—God is Love. You are nourished, renewed, and fulfilled in your Being by that interconnectedness. Yet you are human, a created Being.

> [37] *No, in all these things we are more than conquerors through him who loved us.* [38] *For I am convinced that neither death nor life, neither angels nor demons, neither the present nor the future, nor any powers,* [39] *neither height nor depth, nor anything else in all creation, will be able to separate us from the love of God that is in Christ Jesus our Lord.*
> Romans 8: 37-39

Love conquers all. Neither the past, nor the present, nor the future, nor any powers can separate you from Love.

CHAPTER SIX
THE INNER BODY

BEING IS YOUR DEEPER SELF

In my book, *Five Fold Cycle – Method of Healing Personal Hurt: Healing Life's Hurts,* [1] I explain that you are made of four components: Body, Mind, Soul, and Spirit. These four components are inter-active, each influencing the other. You will remember entanglement mentioned in Chapter One, where in ballet or tango the individual dancers' practice, focus, and tuning allow them to emerge as one. Similarly, the four components cannot be separated, although you can focus on individual components for healing. Sickness in one area affects the other areas negatively; for example, worry might cause ulcers. Health in one area would have positive effects on other areas.

It is understood that the Body is the Temple of the Holy Spirit. The Mind includes old thoughts, patterns & behaviors, memories and the emotions tied to them, and new thoughts and impulses. The Soul is the reservoir for sins and blessings. The Spirit is the component that ties you to Love—God's Spirit.

There Are Four Kinds of Sickness:

- **PHYSICAL SICKNESS** in your body, caused by disease/accidents & other trauma.
- **EMOTIONAL SICKNESS** and problems caused by the emotional hurts of your past.
- **SICKNESS OF SOUL** caused by personal sin.
- **DEMONIC OPPRESSION** caused by spiritual contamination, which may cause any of the above.

There Are Four Corresponding Prayer Methods:

- **PRAYER FOR PHYSICAL HEALING** – Your body exudes the residue of past hurts, accidents, diseases, and trauma.
- **PRAYER FOR INNER HEALING** – Healing of Memories and Emotions resulting from trauma in your life.
- **PRAYER FOR REPENTANCE** (There are 2 steps – Repentance and Forgiveness) – Repentance and Forgiveness are necessary for relief of personal sin.
- **PRAYER FOR DELIVERANCE** – Evil spirits tend to attach to your woundedness and complicate healing.

In *Five Fold Cycle – Method of Healing Personal Hurt: Healing Life's Hurts*, I suggest that you need to be free in each of these areas. *Free from the illusion that you are nothing more than your physical body and your mind.*[2] In Scriptural terms, freedom means healing—mental/emotional, physical, soul, and spiritual healing.

LOOK BEYOND THE WORDS

In answering a question about sin, Eckhart Tolle states, *Over the centuries, many erroneous views and interpretations have accumulated around words such as sin, due to ignorance, misunderstandings, or a desire to control, but they contain an essential core of truth.*[3] He goes on to say that *If you don't like the word sin, then call it unconsciousness or insanity.*[4] In reality, there is a counter argument: your actions affect the world around you, as well as yourself. Injury caused to others or the world around you are sin.

You will remember the phrase that I used earlier: 'Whatever you send out goes out.' If you send out positives, it blesses people. If you send out negativity, it hurts, confounds the world around you, and may destroy people. Your tongue can bless or curse.

FINDING YOUR INVISIBLE AND INDESTRUCTIBLE REALITY

Eckhart Tolle catches the idea of Being in these statements, *But that visible and tangible body is only an outer shell, or rather a limited and distorted perception of a deeper reality.*[5] *Underneath your outer form, you are connected with something so vast, so immeasurable and sacred, that it cannot be conceived or spoken of—yet I am speaking of it now. I am speaking of it not to give you something to believe in but to show you how you can know it for yourself.*[6] From Eckhart Tolle's material you can conclude that if you do not interact with the body, mind, soul, and spirit, then it is most difficult to experience the sacred—Being. Although he would not state this, *underneath your outer form* there is a connection with Love.

Eckhart Tolle goes on to say, *To become conscious of Being, you need to reclaim consciousness from the mind. This is one of the most essential tasks on your spiritual journey.*[7] I would call this Inner Healing, healing the mind; the mind is the battlefield. Eckhart Tolle references healing the mind as freeing *vast amounts of consciousness that previously had been trapped in useless and compulsive thinking.*[8]

CONNECTING WITH THE INNER BODY

Eckhart Tolle invites you to get in touch with your body and get inside your body so that *you may get an image of your body becoming luminous.*[9] He goes on to explain, *The inner body lies at the threshold between your form identity and your essence identity, your true nature. Never lose touch with it.*[10] Is he talking about entering into the Glory? Is he talking about using your body to reach your true nature, the soul? Might he be talking about seeing your aura, when the Glory of God in you becomes visible?

Glory refers to the magnificent display of God's divine presence, power, and perfection, encompassing His worth, radiance, and majesty.

You see, there is the visible and the invisible; there is the body and the soul. You are both *form identity and essence identity*— inseparable. Eckhart Tolle says this is *your true nature. Never lose touch with it.*[11] Although he would not use these words, he is talking about the point of connection between your spirit and the Spirit of Love.

I have found that those with Spiritual Gifts can see Glory. They can tell how connected you are. Glory in you becomes revealed, meaning that Love's magnificence or splendor is being made visible through you, indicating that your actions, character, or life are reflecting the Divine Nature in a way that others can see and experience. In essence this would mean that your life is showcasing Love's Glory through your actions and Being. Interesting!

The dramatic story of Moses' radiant face from Scripture provides some understanding.

> [29] When Moses came down from Mount Sinai with the two tablets of the covenant law in his hands, he was not aware that his face was radiant because he had spoken with the LORD. [30] When Aaron and all the Israelites saw Moses, his face was radiant, and they were afraid to come near him.
> Exodus 34: 29-30

The story of Moses radiating the Glory so that people could see the difference gives an example of how you may radiate Love and how those around you might see it, experience it or sense it. A branch attached to the vine exudes the presence.

TRANSFORMATION THROUGH THE BODY

Eckhart Tolle presents a number of thoughts about man denying his body after the fall of Adam and Eve. Genesis 3 presents the story of Adam and Eve.

> *⁶ When the woman saw that the fruit of the tree was good for food and pleasing to the eye, and also desirable for gaining wisdom, she took some and ate it. She also gave some to her husband, who was with her, and he ate it. ⁷ Then the eyes of both of them were opened, and they realized they were naked; so they sewed fig leaves together and made coverings for themselves.*
> Genesis 3: 6-7

Adam and Eve had eaten the fruit of the tree of the knowledge of good and evil. Their eyes were opened, they were afraid, and they saw that they were naked and covered themselves. Shame entered the world because they had separated themselves from Love. Somehow the body became an obstacle to experiencing Heaven.

Eckhart Tolle states, *The fact is that no one has ever become enlightened through denying or fighting the body... Transformation is through the body, not away from it.*[12] He next frames this argument by stating *Jesus never relinquished his body but remained one with it and ascended into "heaven" with it.*[13] From these statements you understand that you do not lose your body; your body continues to Heaven. Transformation comes with and through your body.

Difficulties arise in the next statements, where Eckhart Tolle expresses again that he is the I am and that you are also the I am. *I am the master, and so are you, once you are able to access the Source within.*[14]

There are problems with those statements. Yes, *all spiritual teachings originate from the same Source.*[15] Yes, there is *only one master.*[16] But no, you are not the I AM! Truth is more than a proposition. Truth is a person—the I AM. (Exodus 3: 14; John 8: 58)

Scripture outlines this fact that Truth is a person.

> [6] Jesus answered, "I am the way and the truth and the life. No one comes to the Father except through me.
> John 14: 6

Jesus, referring to himself as the second person of the Blessed Trinity, states, *I am the way and the truth and the life.* This is a counter argument to Eckhart Tolle's thoughts.

Clarity comes when you consider authority and power. Authority and power come from the I AM. You are subservient to, but not the source of, this authority and power. It's like the Chinese word DE.

> De (/de/; Chinese: 德; pinyin: dé), also written as Te, is a key concept in Chinese philosophy, usually translated as "inherent character; inner power; integrity" in Taoism, "moral character; virtue; morality" in Confucianism and other contexts, and "quality; virtue" (guna) or "merit; virtuous deeds" (punya) in Chinese Buddhism. [17]

De is an inner power, virtue, quality, and inherent character placed within, likened to a plant, but it is not the source, not the I AM. A plant has in it a potential, a power that will develop into something. It is not the source of the potential. The plant cannot call itself the I AM.

SERMON ON THE BODY

You could get lost in all of this loquacity; Eckhart Tolle has a way of piling on extraneous words, thus hiding the true principle.

He states: *the body, which is subject to disease, old age, and death, is not ultimately real—is not you. It is a misperception of your essential reality that is beyond birth and death, and is due to the limitations of your mind, which, having lost touch with Being, creates the body as evidence of its illusory belief in separation and to justify its state of fear. But do not turn away from the body, for within the symbol of impermanence, limitation, and death that you perceive as the illusory creation of your mind is concealed the splendor of your essential and immortal reality.*[18]

What does all that mean? In reality, Eckhart Tolle takes a basic, simple principle of Christian belief, taken from Scripture, and makes it complex. Look at what Scripture said:

> [50] I declare to you, brothers and sisters, that flesh and blood cannot inherit the kingdom of God, nor does the perishable inherit the imperishable.

> [51] Listen, I tell you a mystery: We will not all sleep, but we will all be changed— [52] in a flash, in the twinkling of an eye, at the last trumpet. For the trumpet will sound, the dead will be raised imperishable, and we will be changed. [53] For the perishable must clothe itself with the imperishable, and the mortal with immortality. [54] When the perishable has been clothed with the imperishable, and the mortal with immortality, then the saying that is written will come true: "Death has been swallowed up in victory." [55] "Where, O death, is your victory? Where, O death, is your sting?"
> 1 Corinthians 15: 50-55

Your perishable body in mortality will be clothed in the imperishable, the mortal with immortality. It is more clearly defined in Philippians.

> [21] who, by the power that enables him to bring everything under his control, will transform our lowly bodies so that they will be like his glorious body.
> Philippians 3: 21

In the resurrection of Jesus Christ, you see the transformation of the human body into an immortal body, thus opening the door to your transformation. Scripture clearly explains that your body will be transformed.

The scriptural exegesis from 1 Corinthians 15 gives understanding to resurrection and the transformation of your body.

> [45] So it is written: "The first man Adam became a living Being"; the last Adam, a life-giving spirit. [46] The spiritual did not come first, but the natural, and after that the spiritual. [47] The first man was of the dust of the earth; the second man is of heaven. [48] As was the earthly man, so are those who are of the earth; and as is the heavenly man, so also are those who are of heaven. [49] And just as we have borne the image of the earthly man, so shall we bear the image of the heavenly man. [50] I declare to you, brothers and sisters, that flesh and blood cannot inherit the kingdom of God, nor does the perishable inherit the imperishable. [51] Listen, I tell you a mystery: We will not all sleep, but we will all be changed— [52] in a flash, in the twinkling of an eye, at the last trumpet. For the trumpet will sound, the dead will be raised

> *imperishable, and we will be changed.*
> 1 Corinthians 15: 45-52

Adam was the first; Jesus was the last Adam. Adam was the earthly man; Jesus is heavenly. Jesus' resurrection moved His body from perishable to imperishable. The mystery is that you will change in a flash. The dead will be raised imperishable and will be changed.

Scripture clearly explains that your body will be transformed. This truth is not *a misperception of your essential reality.* This is not *an illusion.*[19] Eckhart Tolle has in fact missed the point—missed the truth.

He does, however, come to a good conclusion in the paragraph to follow. *The art of inner-body awareness will develop into a completely new way of living, the state of permanent connectedness with Being, and will add a depth to your life that you have never known before.*[20]

TO RECAPITULATE: You are learning that the present reality, your body, your mind, your soul, and your spirit are interconnected. You are learning that when *challenges come,* *as they always do,*[21] you are to invite Love's healing and wholeness. You are to be attached like a branch to the vine. The dissonance that you feel in life, is healed by bringing Love's Spirit, through your spirit, into your body, your mind, and your soul. It's a gradual process of becoming one with Love—Being.

The only reason Love exists in the universe is because the Creator of the universe is Love—a Loving God. Love made you. God is Love.

The absence of God is the absence of Love, it is fear. If you reject Love, you are rejecting your identity, your essence; you are rejecting humanity.

The only reason that you can give Love and receive Love, is because you are made in God's image—you are a Love image and a Love maker. You are a manifestation of the mystery of God in you.

Here is a complicated idea that Eckhart Tolle should have presented. The first purpose in life is not to chase Love, not that you are not to love God, but that you are to let God Love you.

[19] We love because he first loved us.
1 John 4: 19

Scripture says you Love because He first loved. You love because He first loved you. You are called to respond to the Love of God. You are to let God love you.

I enjoy how Eckhart Tolle seeds partial truths into his work. In this section, he is discussing when challenges come against you.

If a response is required in that situation, it will come from this deeper level. Just as the sun is infinitely brighter than a candle flame, there is infinitely more intelligence in Being than in your mind.[21]

I wonder if Eckhart Tolle would understand that you, the branch attached to the vine, can have access to Love's intelligence, which is much deeper and infinite than your mind. I enjoy the man!

BEFORE YOU ENTER THE BODY, FORGIVE

In answering a question in this section, Eckhart Tolle explains that the body holds on to emotions: *anger, fear, grief, and so on.*[22] He describes these phenomena as *pain-*

body. He is trying to explain why you may not be able to enter into that peace that passes all understanding, which was referred to in the section *Enlightenment: Rising Above Thought*. He explains the source as, *The pain-body, a parasite that can live inside you for years, feed on your energy, lead to physical illness, and make your life miserable.*[23]

Eckhart Tolle suggests that you should forgive and enter into inner healing; *check whether your mind is holding on to a grievance pattern such as blame, self-pity, or resentment that is feeding the emotion. If that is the case, it means that you haven't forgiven.*[24]

I suggest that you refer to my book, *Five Fold Cycle – Method Of Healing Personal Hurt*. In it you will find a simple method of cleansing and healing these kinds of situations, forgiveness being just one of the many things necessary for healing and wholeness. You might also use my booklet, *Wholeness Through Healing And Forgiveness,* as a resource to help you find and clear memories and trauma from the past.

Forgiveness allows you to experience what Eckhart Tolle refers to as *the vibrant peace and stillness that emanates from Being,*[25] which I refer to as Love.

YOUR LINK WITH THE UNMANIFESTED

Eckhart Tolle explains that *When you have reached a certain stage of inner connectedness, you recognize the truth when you hear it.*[26] In this statement he is giving way to the Scriptural idea that deep within, you have this inner sense, pre-knowledge, and intuition to know the truth.

You can understand this Scriptural teaching by looking at a few Scriptures. First, look at John 8.

> [12] When Jesus spoke again to the people, he said, "I am the light of the world. Whoever follows me will never walk in darkness, but will have the light of life."
> John 8: 12

For you to know the truth, never walk in darkness; to have the light of life, you have to follow Jesus. Remember, Jesus, the second person of the Blessed Trinity, is Love.

Coming after this first step of relationship, inner connectedness, and oneness with Love, is the grace of knowing the truth. In scriptural terms this is discipleship. You might refer again to John 8.

> [31] To the Jews who had believed him, Jesus said, "If you hold to my teaching, you are really my disciples. [32] Then you will know the truth, and the truth will set you free."
> John 8: 31-32

Jesus is essentially saying that true discipleship requires not just initial belief but also actively following His teachings and living according to them, which would lead to a deeper understanding of the truth and ultimate freedom.

Am I stretching Eckhart Tolle's teaching? No! Eckhart Tolle takes from the ancients and imparts his understanding of their messages. The back cover of his book states, *He writes with the timeless and uncomplicated clarity of the ancient spiritual masters and imparts a simple yet profound message: There is a way out of suffering and into peace.*[27]

Are you comfortable with the fact that his message is good but not complete?

SLOWING DOWN THE AGING PROCESS

Eckhart Tolle says, *If you are 20 years old now, the energy field of your inner body will feel just the same when you are eighty. It will be just as vibrantly alive.*[28] He says, *Try it out and you will be the evidence.*[29]

Once again, without acknowledging it, Eckhart Tolle is expressing what ancients have spoken.

> [15] He will renew your life and sustain you in your old age.
> Ruth 4: 15

In Ruth you hear that when a branch is attached to the vine, your life is renewed and you are sustained.

> [4] "Even to your old age and gray hairs I am he, I am he who will sustain you. I have made you and I will carry you; I will sustain you and I will rescue you"
> Isaiah 46: 4

In Isaiah you are told, that you will be sustained in your old age and grey hair, that Love will carry you, sustain you and rescue you.

Now this Scripture will catch you! Are you ready to be 120 years old?

> [7] Moses was a hundred and twenty years old when he died, yet his eyes were not weak nor his strength gone.
> Deuteronomy 34: 7

Moses was 120 when he died, yet he had strength, and his eyes were strong. Life attached to the vine renews and sustains, allowing for a fuller and healthier life.

Eckhart Tolle has caught the message of the ages, that as you 'enter in,' there will be a change, possibly a slowing down of the aging process.

STRENGTHENING THE IMMUNE SYSTEM

Eckhart Tolle is talking about flooding your body with consciousness. As you continually focus your consciousness into your body, you gain a *strengthening of the immune system.*[30] He goes on to say that *the body loves the attention. It is also a potential form of self-healing.*[31]

He goes on to say, *Most illnesses creep in when you are not present in the body. If the master is not present, all kinds of shady characters will take up residence there.*[32]

I think he has taken this idea from Scripture. What does Scripture really say? And what is the underlying meaning of *shady characters?*

In reality, Eckhart Tolle is taking the parable of the 'Strongman' from Scripture, found in both Mark 3: 27 and Matthew 12: 29, and giving you part of the message. The Scripture describes demons being cast out of a house; and upon their return, finding a place empty and coming back with force.

Read through this Scripture talking about the Strongman.

> [23] *So Jesus called them over to him and began to speak to them in parables: "How can Satan drive out Satan?* [24] *If a kingdom is divided against itself, that kingdom cannot stand.* [25] *If a house is divided against itself, that house cannot stand.* [26] *And if Satan opposes himself and is divided, he cannot stand; his end has come.* [27] *In fact, no one can enter a strong man's house without first tying him up. Then he can plunder the strong man's house.*
> Mark 3: 23-27

In this Scripture, people are accusing Jesus of being from Satan. You all know that Satan is the antithesis of Jesus Christ. Like Eckhart Tolle, Mark is stating that if you are full of Being, no one can enter. Being as understood by Scripture as the Holy Spirit who dwells within you.

Eckhart Tolle's reference to *shady characters* is understood as impure spirits or Satan's demons.

> [43] "When an impure spirit comes out of a person, it goes through arid places seeking rest and does not find it. [44] Then it says, 'I will return to the house I left.' When it arrives, it finds the house unoccupied, swept clean and put in order. [45] Then it goes and takes with it seven other spirits more wicked than itself, and they go in and live there. And the final condition of that person is worse than the first. That is how it will be with this wicked generation."
> Matthew 12: 43-45

The impure spirit or *shady characters* will stay outside you, if you are filled with the Holy Spirit, but if you are empty, they will come back with vengeance.

In my book *Five Fold Cycle – Method of Healing Personal Hurt,* I have a drawing that helps image this idea from Eckhart Tolle. The image is called the Human Sieve.

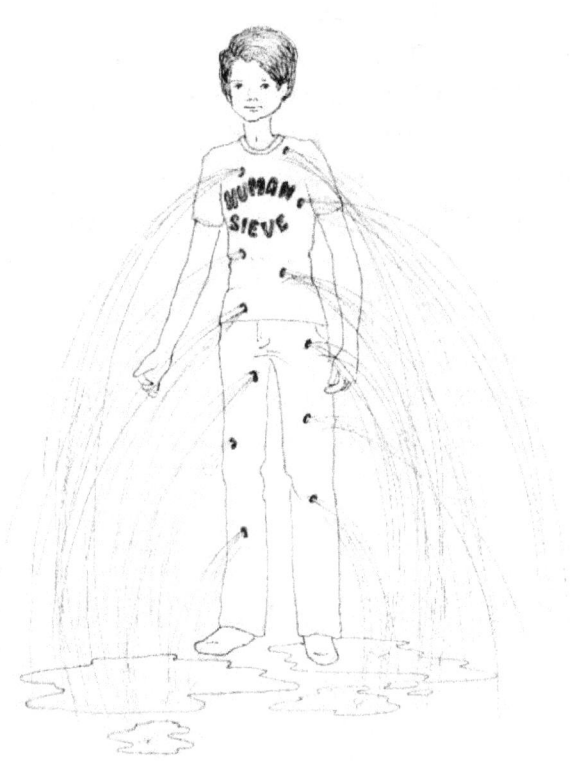

The image shows a boy with all sorts of holes, like a sieve, draining the liquid out of him. The idea is that you are always losing the energy and the grace and need to continually be renewed. Eckhart Tolle states, *when you are unoccupied for a few minutes, and especially last thing at night before you fall asleep and first thing in the morning before getting up, "flood" your body with consciousness.*[33] Eckhart Tolle is talking about flooding your body with consciousness under the title of *Strengthening The Immune System.* He is suggesting you build yourself up, but he is missing the point. In reality, you are to ask for the in-filling of the Holy Spirit to top you up and renew that inner power and potential.

This need to *"flood"* your body is a very important Scriptural message. It will be discussed in the following sections with the phrase, 'Baptism in the Spirit.'

LET THE BREATH TAKE YOU INTO THE BODY

Answering a question from the audience, Eckhart Tolle directs that you should focus on your breathing. He states, *Conscious breathing, which is a powerful meditation in its own right, will gradually put you in touch with the body.*[34] *Then breathe in the light. Feel that luminous substance filling up your body and making it luminous also.*[35]

In reality, without awareness, Eckhart Tolle is sharing an idea from Scripture. In Scripture, breath is a symbol of life and a gift from God—a gift from Love. The word for breath in Hebrew and Greek can also mean spirit or soul. Therefore, when you breathe in, you are breathing in the Holy Spirit. The Holy Spirit gives life.

In Genesis 2, God breathed life into humans, making them living Beings. Breath equates life.

> [7] Then the LORD God formed a man from the dust of the ground and breathed into his nostrils the breath of life, and the man became a living Being.
> Genesis 2: 7

As I present a counter argument to Eckhart Tolle, it is my hope that you gain a deeper understanding of the importance of Scripture as the source of truth. Look at this message from Job.

> [8] But it is the spirit in a person, the breath of the Almighty, that gives them understanding.
> Job 32: 8

Job explains that there is a Spirit within people, the breath of the Almighty within them, *that gives them understanding.* You will remember earlier how it was expressed that through inter-activeness with Love you can engage with intellect and understanding.

The breath of God is the source of wisdom and truth—the source of the Holy Spirit, as expressed in Scripture from John.

> [21] Again Jesus said, "Peace be with you! As the Father has sent me, I am sending you." [22] And with that he breathed on them and said, "Receive the Holy Spirit.
> John 20: 21-22

John 20 says that Jesus breathed on his disciples, proclaiming, "Receive the Holy Spirit." The breath from Love pours out the Holy Spirit onto you. Job brings the teaching back to its source; Love gives life, intellect, and understanding, and Love is the Creator.

> [4] The Spirit of God has made me; the breath of the Almighty gives me life.
> Job 33: 4

Job teaches that the Spirit of God has made you, and Love's breath—the breath of the Almighty—gives you life. Will you betray Love—the source of breath and life?

These Scriptural truths can only bring you to praise.

> ⁶ Let everything that has breath praise the LORD.
> Psalm 150: 6

Will you praise Love? Will your breath be praise?

CREATIVE USE OF MIND
Eckhart Tolle is encouraging you to listen, both through your body and your mind, to expand the way you process. *We could say, Don't just think with your head, think with your whole body.*³⁶ You will remember that there are four components body, mind, soul, and spirit—acting inter-actively. As they are all inter-active, the *Creative Use Of Mind* comes through using all four areas to open and listen.

THE ART OF LISTENING
*When listening to another person, don't just listen with your mind, listen with your whole body. Feel the energy field of your inner body as you listen.*³⁶ Eckhart Tolle is encouraging you to *feel someone else's Being* through your own.³⁸ He goes on to say that *At the deepest level of Being, you are one with all*

that is.[39] You are one with all of humanity, each made in the image of God, each sharing the indwelling Holy Spirit. The Holy Spirit helps you to be one with each other and one with God.

The Scriptural principle is that you are one body in Christ. It is a wonderful message of Love's design.

> **Unity and Diversity in the Body**
> [12] Just as a body, though one, has many parts, but all its many parts form one body, so it is with Christ. [13] For we were all baptized by one Spirit so as to form one body—whether Jews or Gentiles, slave or free—and we were all given the one Spirit to drink. [14] Even so the body is not made up of one part but of many. [15] Now if the foot should say, "Because I am not a hand, I do not belong to the body," it would not for that reason stop being part of the body. [16] And if the ear should say, "Because I am not an eye, I do not belong to the body," it would not for that reason stop being part of the body. [17] If the whole body were an eye, where would the sense of hearing be? If the whole body were an ear, where would the sense of

smell be? ¹⁸ But in fact God has placed the parts in the body, every one of them, just as he wanted them to be. ¹⁹ If they were all one part, where would the body be? ²⁰ As it is, there are many parts, but one body.
1 Corinthians 12: 12-20

You are one body with diverse parts, designed and created by Love.

CHAPTER SEVEN
PORTALS INTO THE UNMANIFESTED

GOING DEEPLY INTO THE BODY

Eckhart Tolle is encouraging you to get into a meditative state, relax, close your eyes, quiet your mind, be attentive to your body's rhythms, and find that inner peace—*inner energy field of the body.*[1] Let yourself go and enter in. He calls the state that you enter into *the Unmanifested, the invisible Source of all things, the Being within all Beings. It is a realm of deep stillness and peace, but also of joy and intense aliveness.*[2]

Eckhart Tolle drops new words into your vocabulary. He makes it sound like there is something new and wonderful. In reality these ideas are wonderful, but they are not new; they are a presentation of the old. Many forms of meditative states encourage relaxation, quieting, and entering into that inner peace. They include Centering Prayer, Scripture-Centered Worship Music, Breath Prayer, and Regular or Guided Meditations.

I am wondering if you might be feeling an underlying tension as you read this material? Does the scriptural truth contrast with what you have read from Eckhart Tolle? Scripture and truth are an antidote for New Age rhetoric.

New Age rhetoric tends to promote self-improvement, spiritual self-transformation, and a belief in the ability to heal oneself. It often combines ideas from many different cultural and spiritual traditions. It contends that you have everything in yourselves necessary to achieve fulfillment—transcendence. It is self-interest-based, tending to encourage self-focus. It also hints that all perspectives on the divine are equally valid. These all sound like good things. This flow of thought brings you to the idea that you are the primary source of spiritual authority—you become God—you become Love. This is the conundrum once again.

Scripture frames the picture differently. Scripture puts Jesus, the Christ, at the center. As you lean into Scripture and form a relationship with Love, as a branch to the vine, you find out that New Age rhetoric is flawed. Scripture and truth are the antidote.

In the Christian frame of reference, '*apart-ed-ness*' means submission to the authority, from which you get your spiritual power—De. It is a share, participation, with Love. Love being the source of authority and power. Nothing is more powerful than Love.

This is the Good News. Love is mystical, supernatural. Love is catholic—universal. It manifests visibly, in that you can see the glow on people. You are drawn to those people. My encouragement is that you seek Love!

THE SOURCE OF THAT CHI

The Unmanifested is the source of chi. Chi is the inner energy field of your body. It is a bridge between the outer you and the Source. It lies halfway between the manifested, the world of form, and the Unmanifested. Chi can be likened to a river or an energy stream.[3] What might Eckhart Tolle be talking about in that statement? He is talking about looking deep into the inner body, looking for the Unmanifested. He describes the Unmanifested—*the Unmanifested takes on form as the energy stream of chi...*[4]

Eckhart Tolle, without knowing it, is talking about accessing the Rivers of Living Water described in John 7.

> [37] *On the last and greatest day of the festival, Jesus stood and said in a loud*

> voice, "Let anyone who is thirsty come to me and drink. [38] Whoever believes in me, as Scripture has said, rivers of living water will flow from within them." [39] By this he meant the Spirit, whom those who believed in him were later to receive. Up to that time the Spirit had not been given, since Jesus had not yet been glorified.
> John 7: 37-39

In the Scripture, Apostle John is quoting Jesus, who is talking about the Rivers of Living Water that reside in your belly. What are these, Rivers? What is this energy stream? In Scripture, Jesus is referring to the Holy Spirit that resides in the temple of your body, when you are joined to the vine.

There is even more information in Scripture.

> [13] For we were all baptized by one Spirit so as to form one body—whether Jews or Gentiles, slave or free—and we were all given the one Spirit to drink.
> 1 Corinthians 12:13

Scripture says, you and all of humanity, are baptized by one Spirit, the Holy Spirit; that you were given the one Spirit to drink. You will remember that Scripture has been referring to the Holy Spirit as Rivers of Living Water. These rivers join you with anyone connected to the Holy Spirit, making you one body, one body in Christ. You see how this message is much deeper in its scriptural exegesis.

The Unmanifested that Eckhart Tolle is describing is the Rivers of Living Water—the power of the Holy Spirit that resides within. Without giving you the full understanding of the Scripture, He is inviting you to connect with this force. The New Age rhetoric does not add to this historical Scripture and truth that is available to you.

(Learn about the Rivers of Living Water by reading Appendix A.)

DREAMLESS SLEEP
You take a journey into the Unmanifested every night when you enter the phase of deep dreamless sleep. You merge with the Source.[5]

Scripture says it quite poetically, that Love speaks to you in your dreams.

> [14] For God does speak—now one way, now another—though no one perceives it. [15] In a dream, in a

> vision of the night, when deep sleep falls on people as they slumber in their beds, ¹⁶ he may speak in their ears and terrify them with warnings, ¹⁷ to turn them from wrongdoing and keep them from pride, ¹⁸ to preserve them from the pit, their lives from perishing by the sword.
> Job 33: 14-18

Through dreams, Love speaks to you, offering guidance, discernment, and counsel to your life and decisions.

The Acts of the Apostles in Scripture elaborates.

> ¹⁷ "'In the last days, God says, I will pour out my Spirit on all people. Your sons and daughters will prophesy, your young men will see visions, your old men will dream dreams.
> Acts 2: 17

Love pours out His Spirit on all mankind. Your children will prophesy, young men will see visions, and you will dream dreams. This is a clear message, a clear truth, that Love offers you regular, continual, true, and consistent interaction and connection. It is left to you to open the door and access the rivers.

In my first book, I presented a picture taken from circa 1883, titled 'Christ Before Thy Door Is Waiting' by W. Rainey.

The painting shows Christ standing outside the old solid door and knocking. There is no visible latch or doorknob. It becomes obvious to say that the knock at the door requires someone from within to respond. The artist is implying that you must open the door. Turning to Love requires using your free will to open yourself to the Love. The artist implies that Love waits patiently, arms outstretched, with love flowing. All that you need to do is open the door a little way or throw it wide open. It's up to you to choose.

> [9] *"So I say to you: Ask and it will be given to you; seek and you will find; knock and the door will be opened to you.* [10] *For everyone who asks receives; the one who seeks finds; and to the one who knocks, the door will be opened.*
> Luke 11: 9-10

Asking for Love, seeking Love, and knocking on Love's door are all choices helping you to find, receive, and enter into Love.

OTHER PORTALS

Eckhart Tolle, without acknowledging the Scripture, is encouraging you to fully access love. He mentions the Now is the main portal, where you *dissolve psychological time*.[6] *The cessation of thinking... that there is no mental commentary running*, is another portal.[7] *Surrender—the letting go of mental-*

emotional resistance to what is—also becomes a portal into the Unmanifested. [8] Eckhart Tolle goes on to say that it's up to you to open the portals in your life, to *get in touch with the energy field of the inner body.*[9] His final summary is that *your task is not to search for love but to find a portal through which love can enter.*[10]

Do you find it odd that both Eckhart Tolle and I have stated the same idea: your task is not to search for love but to be open to receive? Eckhart Tolle and I approach it from different foundations. He writes on the back cover that he uses *the timeless and uncomplicated clarity of the ancient spiritual masters and imparts a simple yet profound message.*[11] In reality, Eckhart Tolle has taken portions of Scripture, applied his own terms like *Unmanifested*, and presented a bill of goods, which has caught the eye of many. His book purports that he sold over two million copies.

Let me do a review for you to help give clarity.

You will have noticed by now that Eckhart Tolle is using three words—essence, Being, and presence—interchangeably. You will have also noted that I have added Love to the group of words. Love meaning God and God meaning the three persons of the Blessed Trinity: Father, Son, and Holy Spirit.

Periodically, I have used Creator for God the Father—who is Love and the Great I AM. This is a significant change from the New Age rhetoric. This new rhetoric transposes the message from New Age to Christian. The counter argument is that Eckhart Tolle presents only part of the picture and that the Scriptural foundation gives you the complete message necessary to find that inner peace, that tranquility, and to find Love.

In these pages, I have led you to a more complete exegesis; it is the Christian understanding of living in Christ expressed as Love.

The exegesis of Love might go like this. The first purpose in life is not to chase Love, not that you are not to love God, but that you are to let God Love you.

First John from Scripture explains why you are to let God love you.

> [19] *We love because he first loved us.*
> 1 John 4: 19

Scripture states that you Love because He first loved. You love out of His Love. You are called to respond to the Love of God. My encouragement is that you seek Love!

This is the Good News. Love is mystical, supernatural. Love is catholic—universal. It manifests visibly, in that you can see the glow on people. You are drawn to those people. You are called to know the truth, never walk in darkness, have the light of life, to follow Love. Remember, God is Love.

Emanating from this initial experience of interconnectedness, relationship, and oneness with Love, is the grace of knowing the truth. In scriptural terms this is discipleship. You will remember a previous reference to John 8.

> [31] To the Jews who had believed him, Jesus said, "If you hold to my teaching, you are really my disciples. [32] Then you will know the truth, and the truth will set you free."
> John 8: 31-32

The relationship with Love offers a New Life. This relationship with Love gives you the knowledge of the truth, the truth will give you true freedom.

> [4] The Spirit of God has made me; the breath of the Almighty gives me life.
> Job 33: 4

You will remember reading earlier that Job 33: 4 teaches that the Spirit of God has made you, and Love's breath—the breath of the Almighty—gives you life. Love is inside you. Love is the Creator. Love has been within you before you were born, as it says in Jeremiah.

> [5] "Before I formed you in the womb I knew[a] you, before you were born I set you apart; I appointed you as a prophet to the nations."
> Jeremiah 1: 5
> Footnotes
> [a] *chose*

Love knew you before your creation, formed you in your mother's womb, and *set you apart,* (apart-ed-ness), as a unique individual. There will be no other like you. You have your unique fingerprint, your own DNA string, and your own iris biometric. Love has appointed you to this time, this particular place, and this present life.

Your job is to lean in to Love, open to Love in your body, mind, soul, and spirit. Eckhart Tolle would have you in the Now. Love would have you in a relationship, always in union with Love, whether you are healing the past, ruminating about the future, or dreaming, you are to be one with Love. It is all about relationship.

SILENCE

It has been said that nothing in this world is so like God as silence.[12] Eckhart Tolle has caught an important thought: that silence is a significant opening to God. He calls it a portal, a way of opening. *Silence without, stillness within.*[13]

SPACE

Eckhart Tolle writes about portals, like silence and space, that help you enter into the Unmanifested. What does he mean by Unmanifested? You know that manifest means that something has become evident or certain by being shown or displayed. Unmanifested then means that this presence or Being, as Eckhart Tolle describes it, is hidden. I would suggest that Unmanifest would best be defined as the indwelling Holy Spirit and Love.

What Eckhart Tolle suggests is that you position yourself in a quiet place, a space away from distraction. Scripture gives depth to this idea.

> ⁶ But when you pray, go into your room, close the door and pray to your Father, who is unseen. Then your Father, who sees what is done in secret, will reward you.
> Matthew 6: 6

Go into your room, find a space away from distraction, and close the door. Open yourself, pray to God the Father, and you will be rewarded. The reward is the manifestation experienced in that quiet space, an interior connection with Love. Eckhart Tolle calls this *the appearance of the Unmanifested*.[14]

He goes on in his loquacity and garrulity to write about space being the same as nothing, no-thing, no-mind, and *the infinitely creative womb of all existence*.[15] His complexity does not help. Eckhart Tolle is taking this principle from Scripture and presenting it as: take time away, find that place, that quiet space; make sure there is quiet in that place, because in the quiet of your prayer room, you will be rewarded. What he doesn't say is that in doing this, it will open you to the Holy Spirit and Love.

THE TRUE NATURE OF SPACE AND TIME

Eckhart Tolle writes about space and time, asking the question, *Where did it come from?* [16] He concludes that it comes from *the Unmanifested—the One.*[17] He said there was nothing before. He goes on to describe the universe with the billions of stars and comments, *Yet what is even more awe-inspiring is the infinity of space itself.*[18]

Eckhart Tolle, without giving credence, is describing creation from Scripture. Why would he not bring you to Scripture and its truth?

> [1] *In the beginning God created the heavens and the earth.* [2] *Now the earth was formless and empty, darkness was over the surface of the deep, and the Spirit of God was hovering over the waters.*
> Genesis 1: 1-2

Scripture presents the Creation Story: in the beginning there was void. From the void was created light, Genesis verse 3. Next, in verses 4-5, light was separated from day, day from night. In verses 6-9, there was the separation of water from the sky and the land from the sea. It is an amazing story of creation from the void—*no-thing* as Eckhart Tolle termed it. I enjoy how he coins new words!

Can you learn about Love—the Creator—from Eckhart Tolle? He presents a confusing message: *What you perceive externally as space and time are ultimately illusory, but they contain a core of truth. They are the two essential attributes of God, infinity and eternity...*[19] Unfortunately, Eckhart Tolle is not leading you to God, but God is the Creator, and God is Love.

Next, from Eckhart Tolle, you learn, *within you, both space and time have an inner equivalent that reveals their true nature, as well as your own. Whereas space is the still, infinitely deep realm of no-mind, the inner equivalent of time is presence, awareness of the external Now.*[20] In his loquacity he is missing the mark. In you, in your temple, resides a presence, the Rivers of Living Water, which you have come to know as the Holy Spirit. This is the same Holy Spirit that hovered over the waters at creation (Genesis 1: 2). Eckhart Tolle gives you part of the story, and Scripture fills in the blanks. Love is the source of Creation.

> [2] Before the mountains were born or you brought forth the whole world, from everlasting to everlasting you are God.
> **Psalm 90: 2**

Scripture presents Moses's words explaining that God existed before the universe and that He is outside the universe and beyond the physical laws that govern it.

> [16] For in him all things were created: things in heaven and on earth, visible and invisible, whether thrones or powers or rulers or authorities; all things have been created through him and for him. [17] He is before all things, and in him all things hold together.
> **Colossians 1: 16-17**

From Scripture, you gain the truth, the complete picture, that you are connected in a special way to the Creator. Within you is a hole, only satisfied by the infusion of Love. As you lean into Love, you enter into relationship, like a branch to a vine, you are nourished. These are old truths, found in Christianity.

I have conflict with Eckhart Tolle's next statement. *Hence, the ultimate purpose of the world lies not within the world but in transcendence of the world… You are here to enable the divine purpose of the universe to unfold. That is how important you are!* [21] Possibly Eckhart Tolle has lost his spiritual compass, the GPS that helps him find direction and meaning in life.

Scripture would frame it differently. To God, the earth, His creation, is important and must be cared for. In Genesis God commands people to work it and care for it.

> [15] The LORD God took the man and put him in the Garden of Eden to work it and take care of it.
> **Genesis 2: 15**

Further, Scripture says that God created the earth for a purpose, and that purpose is His glory.

> [1] The heavens declare the glory of God; the skies proclaim the work of his hands. [2] Day after day they pour forth speech; night after night they reveal knowledge.
> **Psalm 19: 1-2**

> ³⁶ For from him and through him and for him are all things. To him be the glory forever! Amen.
> Romans 11: 36

The heavens, the skies, day and night, declare His glory and reveal knowledge of Him. The earth is God's possession; the skies proclaim His handiwork.

> ¹⁴ To the LORD your God belong the heavens, even the highest heavens, the earth and everything in it.
> Deuteronomy 10: 14

Through His creation, Love makes Himself known to humankind. Through everything He made, the earth and sky, you can see His invisible qualities—His eternal power and divine nature.

> ²⁰ For since the creation of the world God's invisible qualities—his eternal power and divine nature—have been clearly seen, being understood from what has been made, so that people are without excuse.
> Romans 1: 20

You have no excuse for not knowing God—Love. His creation clearly presents His divine Nature—God is Love.

> ^{24} but let the one who boasts boast about this: that they have the understanding to know me, that I am the Lord, who exercises kindness, justice and righteousness on earth, for in these I delight," declares the Lord.
> Jeremiah 9: 24

Through Scripture you can know Love, who delights in justice, righteousness, and kindness. Love delights in exercising kindness, justice, and righteousness on earth.

> ^{16} The highest heavens belong to the Lord, but the earth he has given to mankind.
> Psalm 115: 16

God designed you to live on earth, and He has given a specific design to His creation.

> ^{26} From one man he made all the nations, that they should inhabit the whole earth; and he marked out their appointed times in history and the boundaries of their lands.
> Acts 17: 26

As His creation, you are not an accident. You are created for this specific time, in this specific place and history. You are appointed to live in this physical world. You will remember Genesis's description of creation.

> [26] Then God said, "Let us make mankind in our image, in our likeness, so that they may rule over the fish in the sea and the birds in the sky, over the livestock and all the wild animals, and over all the creatures that move along the ground." [27] So God created mankind in his own image, in the image of God he created them; male and female he created them. [28] God blessed them and said to them, "Be fruitful and increase in number; fill the earth and subdue it. Rule over the fish in the sea and the birds in the sky and over every living creature that moves on the ground."
> **Genesis 1: 26-28**

God made you in His own image, male or female, **saying** be fruitful and increase in number **and** fill the earth and subdue it, giving you dominion over creation. He blessed you, **saying**, Be fruitful and increase in number.

In His design, everything about your bodies is designed to interact with the physical realm and be sustained by the rich earth, the plant life, and the animals.

God places you on this earth for His sovereign good.

> ⁶ The LORD does whatever pleases him, in the heavens and on the earth, in the seas and all their depths.
> Psalm 135: 6

The Lord's are the heavens and earth, the seas and all their depths. His original design and divine purpose for you is to *fill the earth; the earth He has given to mankind.* Your purpose in this earthly life is to come to know God through a relationship with Jesus Christ.

> ²³ Jesus replied, "Anyone who loves me will obey my teaching. My Father will love them, and we will come to them and make our home with them.
> John 14: 23

When you open to Jesus, you open to the Father, and the Holy Spirit will take up residence within you; *we will come to them and make our home with them.* John 14 is referring to the fact that this residence is in the present, here and now.

> [12] Yet to all who did receive him, to those who believed in his name, he gave the right to become children of God— [13] children born not of natural descent, nor of human decision or a husband's will, but born of God.
> John 1: 12-13

You become an adopted child of Love, born from on high. Through your adoption you gain access to the rights and power of the Godhead. Your purpose is expressed in 1 Corinthians and Colossians.

> [31] So whether you eat or drink or whatever you do, do it all for the glory of God.
> 1 Corinthians 10: 31

> [17] And whatever you do, whether in word or deed, do it all in the name of the Lord Jesus, giving thanks to God the Father through him.
> Colossians 3: 17

In everything you do, you are to glorify Him in this world. You are to do all for His glory. In that relationship, you will be blessed by becoming closer to the Vine. Give thanks.

SECOND RECAPITULATION: To this point in the document, you have been exposed to a contrast between the writings of Erkhart Tolle and Scripture. As author, I have often used the phrase 'in reality,' referencing the fact that Eckhart Tolle has given you a good word, thought, or concept, but not given you its complete exegesis, its complete depth.

I have gradually moved you from the word Love, to God is Love, and finally God meaning the three persons of the Blessed Trinity: Father, Son, and Holy Spirit. You have noted that I refer to God, as the Creator, the I AM, the vine, the presence, and the Blessed Trinity; all are Christian labels.

A personal relationship with Jesus, Jesus the Christ, the Anointed One, is suggested. As author, I suggest that you receive the 'Baptism in the Holy Spirit' and ask for the indwelling of the Holy Spirit. From within your body, the Temple of God, the Holy Spirit will begin to manifest in you the Gifts found in Isaiah 11 and 1 Corinthians 12. These manifestations will open you to Prophecy, Discernment of Spirits, Tongues, Interpretation of Tongues, Word of Knowledge and Word of Wisdom, Faith, Healing and Miracles; encouraging

Understanding, Counsel, Fortitude, Piety and an Awe of the Lord. It is a wonderful journey of relationship, growth, and development.

You are to enter into the 'flow' of the Holy Spirit, the Rivers of Living Water. You are to allow the Holy Spirit to guide and to lead. In doing so you will experience Love's manifestations, right now and right here on earth.

Knowing Christ has changed my life. It has given me a peace that I never had before. It has given me a refuge in times of trouble and a clear moral compass to guide my days. In my 26 years of work as a Christian Counsellor and in the present ministry, the indwelling Holy Spirit has given me the manifestations to help and heal God's people. Each day this relationship with Father, Son, and Holy Spirit opens new doors; Heaven on Earth becomes more tangible.

I invite you to follow the direction of Saint Peter in Acts, where he is talking about the crucifixion and resurrection of Jesus.

> [37] When the people heard this, they were cut to the heart and said to Peter and the other apostles, "Brothers, what shall we do?" [38] Peter replied, "Repent and be

> baptized, every one of you, in the name of Jesus Christ for the forgiveness of your sins. And you will receive the gift of the Holy Spirit. [39] The promise is for you and your children and for all who are far off—for all whom the Lord our God will call."
> Acts 2: 37-39

You are being called! Repent, and be baptized in the name of Jesus Christ for the forgiveness of your sins. Ask for the promise from the Father—His Holy Spirit. Christians call this the 'Laying on of Hands' or the 'Baptism in the Holy Spirit.' This *promise is for you and your children and for all who are far off—for all whom the Lord your God will call.*

(Learn about the Baptism in the Spirit by reading Appendix D.)

CONSCIOUS DEATH
The next portal described by Eckhart Tolle is physical death. He talks briefly about near-death experiences as an example of entering into what might be called the celestial heaven. He states, *One last portal will open up for you immediately after the body has died.* [22] He goes on to say *approaching death*

and death itself, the dissolution of the physical form, is always a great opportunity for spiritual realization.[23] The last statement on the page is interesting. *Every portal is a portal of death, the death of the false self. When you go through it, you cease to derive your identity from your psychological, mind-made form. You then realize that death is an illusion, just as your identification with form was an illusion. The end of the illusion—that's all that death is. It is painful only as long as you cling to illusion.*[24]

In reality, Eckhart Tolle has missed the point. Yes, death is the end of the physical body until you receive your imperishable body. You will remember 1 Corinthians 15: 50-55 and Philippians 3: 21, where Scripture presented the message of transformation and resurrection. Your perishable body in mortality, will be clothed in the imperishable, the mortal with immortality. God, who is Love, has everything under His control and will transform your lowly body so that it will be like His glorious body.

Eckhart Tolle continually tells you that he is *a contemporary spiritual teacher who is not aligned with any particular religion or tradition.*[25] In reality, he takes portions of Christian principles and truths, at a time when people in the world were running away from church and institutions, and presents them as timeless messages, ancient truths, that he says would lead you to *The Power of Now*. In reality, *The Power of Now* means entering into Love—a relationship with Love. The rest of the story is that *The Power of Now is Love.*

CHAPTER EIGHT
ENLIGHTENED RELATIONSHIPS

ENTER THE NOW FROM WHEREVER YOU ARE

I enjoy this man's writing; it makes me smile. This section posed a question from someone stating, *I always thought that true enlightenment is not possible except through love in a relationship between a man and a woman. Isn't this what makes us whole again?*[1] Eckhart Tolle responds, *Is that true in your experience?*[2] I am sure this interplay left you and everyone else cracking a smile, as you know marital relations are difficult.

Eckhart Tolle goes on to say, *In other words, you are waiting for an event in time to save you. Is this not the core error that we had been talking about? Salvation is not elsewhere in place or time. It is here and now.*[3] He is suggesting that people are looking for pleasures in the physical realm and that this gratification shall give them the happiness and satisfaction. Further, he states, *this is the unconscious mind-set that creates the illusion of salvation in the future. True salvation is fulfillment, peace, life in all its fullness. It is to be who you are, to feel within you the good that has no opposite, the joy of Being that depends on nothing outside itself.*[4] Eckhart Tolle has some of it right, but like in the previous chapters, it is not complete and possibly skewed. Let me explain.

The hole that you are trying to fill, that emptiness that you're trying to gratify, is that Love-shaped hole you read about earlier. It needs to be filled with the indwelling Holy Spirit.

You are to be led by the Holy Spirit. What does that mean? Being led has to do with what or whom you are paying attention to. Are you paying attention to pain, what Eckhart Tolle calls *pain-body*, those drivers from the past? Are you paying attention to the present time and place? Are you focusing your attention towards the future? These are all questions Eckhart Tolle suggests block your ability to be in *The Power of Now*. But contrast this to the Scripture from Romans, which talks about the Power of Spirit, the Power of Love.

> [14] For those who are led by the Spirit of God are the children of God. [15] The Spirit you received does not make you slaves, so that you live in fear again; rather, the Spirit you received brought about your adoption to sonship. And by him we cry, *"Abba,* Father." [16] The Spirit

himself testifies with our spirit that we are God's children.
Romans 8: 14-16

What Saint Paul in Romans is saying, is that you are to be led by the Spirit, the Holy Spirit, Love's Spirit. You have learned that Love can dwell within you, in your temple. And you have learned that Love manifests with many gifts including, Understanding, Wisdom, Knowledge, and Discernment. They become available to you as an adopted child of God. Leaning into these will bring blessing in your life and give you peace that passes all understanding. It is all about relationship with Love, God is Love.

As author I would like to pose a few questions that seem apparent from the above paragraph. Are you interested in being a child of God? Would you invite Love to dwell within? Could you join in the relationship with God who is love?

Eckhart Tolle goes on to say that if you are led by a pain-body like fear, then fear is in control, and you will experience sadness, loneliness, depression, and such negatives. If you are a child of fear, you will be driven by insecurity and doubt. If you are led to search and yearn for the future, then you will always feel an emptiness, because you are unfulfilled. If you are stuck on worrying about the present—money, vehicle, mortgage, and job—you will be driven to ulcers and heartache. This portion of Eckhart Tolle's message is correct, but in reality, there is more.

Scripture points to something else that should be leading you; you should be led by the Spirit, the Holy Spirit. Being led by the Spirit means you are a child of God. Notice it is being led, not pushed, not manipulated, not a slave, but led by a loving Father—Abba. A loving Father does not impose His will on you; there is free will.

"Abba" is an Aramaic word found in Scripture meaning "Father," used by Jesus and Paul to address God. It implies a profound intimacy and love, reflecting a filial bond with God—who is Love, not just a distant relationship with the Creator.

You are a child of whatever is leading you. Whatever is leading you is shaping you. If you are led by your emotions, you will always be stuck in an endless spinning of depression, confusion, worry, bitterness, and negativity.

Being a child of God means the Holy Spirit is God in you, leading you. God in you is Love,

Love manifesting. This Scripture from Ephesians encourages this practice.

> [1] Follow God's example, therefore, as dearly loved children [2] and walk in the way of love, just as Christ loved us and gave himself up for us as a fragrant offering and sacrifice to God.
> **Ephesians 5: 1-2**

The benefit to you is that you will be led to come closer, encouraged to open wider, and be more loving, joyful, peaceful, patient, and gentle and have more self-control. All these are manifestations of the Holy Spirit; God is manifesting Himself through you.

These qualities that you will experience are described in the Scripture to Galatians as the fruit of the Holy Spirit.

> [22] But the fruit of the Spirit is love, joy, peace, forbearance, kindness, goodness, faithfulness, [23] gentleness and self-control. Against such things there is no law. [24] Those who belong to Christ Jesus have crucified the flesh with its passions and desires. [25] Since we live by the Spirit, let us keep in step with the Spirit.
> **Galatians 5: 22-25**

You will note that I have expanded Eckhart Tolle's message to encourage you to hear and attain the fullness of Scripture. The benefits to you, in following the lead of the Holy Spirit, are that you will experience Love's fruit: love, joy, peace, patience, kindness, goodness, faithfulness, gentleness, and self-control. Are these qualities that you desire?

LOVE/HATE RELATIONSHIPS

Eckhart Tolle states, *Unless and until you access the consciousness frequency of presence, all relationships, and particularly intimate relationships, are deeply flawed and ultimately dysfunctional.*[5] He states that they will *become love/hate relationships before long.*[6] He sees all relationships as having a positive and negative side, therefore dysfunctional. He also writes about the negativity of divorce leading to jealousy, possessiveness, blaming, and accusing. He makes statements like, *Where is the love now? Can love change into its opposite in an instant? Was it love in the first place, or just an addictive grasping and clinging?*[7]

In all of his rhetoric, you can see that Eckhart Tolle does not see the complete picture. Without the Holy Spirit indwelling, you are left to the world, the flesh, and the devil. This is a complicated message, but let me give you some depth.

> ¹⁵ Do not love the world or anything in the world. If anyone loves the world, love for the Father is not in them. ¹⁶ For everything in the world—the lust of the flesh, the lust of the eyes, and the pride of life—comes not from the Father but from the world. ¹⁷ The world and its desires pass away, but whoever does the will of God lives forever.
> 1 John 2: 15-17

The exegesis of this paragraph is that you are to be in the Father, one with the I AM, like a branch attached to the vine. You receive from the Father His gift, the indwelling Holy Spirit. You no longer look to the world for your fulfillment but to the Father, to Love. In looking to the Father, you escape the lust of the flesh and sexual perversions. You escape the lust of the eyes, which would be greed and covetousness. And you escape the pride of life, which would simply be described as pride. You are no longer looking for things of the world, like your marriage, to fulfill you. You enjoy the things of the world and relationships through the lead of the Holy Spirit, who will bring blessing to you and to things around you and situations around you. Choose to join in relationship with Love.

ADDICTION AND THE SEARCH FOR WHOLENESS

In this chapter, Eckhart Tolle writes about the romantic love relationship and its addictive characteristic. He says that although it is attractive, it does not fill your deep-felt need. *The reason why the romantic love relationship is such an intense and universally sought-after experience is that it seems to offer liberation from a deep-seated state of fear, need, lack, and incompleteness that is part of the human condition in its unredeemed and unenlightened state.*[8]

He goes on to say *The root of this physical urge is a spiritual one: the longing for an end to duality, and return to the state of wholeness. Sexual union is the closest you can get to this state on the physical level.*[9]

Those statements ring true and probably make sense to you. He continues, saying, *on the psychological level, the sense of lack and incompleteness is, if anything, even greater than on the physical level.*[10] Again, this rings true.

Eckhart Tolle compares this romantic attraction to the attraction of an addict addicted to *alcohol, food, legal or illegal drugs.*[11] He states that you are merely addicted to a person and that in this addiction, *you are using something or somebody to cover up your pain.*[12] Further, he explains, *every addiction reaches a point where it does not work for you anymore, and then you feel the pain more intensely than ever. This is one reason why most people are always trying to escape from the present moment and are seeking some kind of salvation in the future.*[13] Eckhart Tolle suggests that you focus on the Now, the power of the presence, so that this focus dissolves pain.

Eckhart Tolle describes a broken world with broken relationships that can only be resolved by becoming one with Being—living in the Now. I have a different solution: that you join with the power and the presence of the Rivers of Living Water; they can change the world around you.

Although there is brokenness in the world, the God I know is a God who cares for me and enjoys a relationship with me. The relationship is intimate and fulfilling. This relationship with God is not something that is forced. It is a relationship of real true Love.

His love enters into every event and interaction I have in the world, Love flowing with Rivers of Living Water.

There is a confidence, a lasting Love. Now God is inside you—the indwelling Holy Spirit. God within offers a deeper personal relationship. This God of History yearns to be in relationship with you.

Nothing can separate you from Love. Love is forever; it is eternal.

> 38 For I am convinced that neither death nor life, neither angels nor demons, neither the present nor the future, nor any power, 39 neither height nor depth, nor anything else in all creation, will be able to separate us from the love of God that is in Christ Jesus our Lord.
> Romans 8: 38-39

You are offered real freedom. God did not make a sick world. God made you in His image with real freedom and real choice. So, if you say no to God, God will honor that choice. A tyrant would not allow free choice, but the God of Love is open to relationship, friendship, mercy, and care. He reveals Himself as a benevolent God. Would you like to be in His company? My answer would be, Yes! A resounding yes!

Put on the new self by renewing your mind, focusing on Love, and becoming connected to the source of life—the True Vine.

> [10] and have put on the new self, which is being renewed in knowledge in the image of its Creator. [11] Here there is no Gentile or Jew, circumcised or uncircumcised, barbarian, Scythian, slave or free, but Christ is all, and is in all. [12] Therefore, as God's chosen people, holy and dearly loved, clothe yourselves with compassion, kindness, humility, gentleness and patience. [13] Bear with each other and forgive one another if any of you has a grievance against someone. Forgive as the Lord forgave you. [14] And over all these virtues put on love, which binds them all together in perfect unity. [15] Let the peace of Christ rule in your hearts, since as members of one body you were called to peace. And be thankful.
> Colossians 3: 10-15

Eckhart Tolle has not totally missed it; his compass is a bit off course. As you read in

Colossians, you are encouraged to *put on a new self*, to open to Love. All humanity is welcome. The brokenness of humanity and the world is transformed by your flow of the Rivers of Living Water. You are encouraged to forgive, bearing nothing against one another. With your connection to the Vine, you manifest Love to the world, *which binds them all together in perfect unity*. Love is attractive like a magnet. People begin to say, "I want what you have." Your job is to introduce them to Love.

FROM ADDICTIVE TO ENLIGHTENED RELATIONSHIPS

Eckhart Tolle confirms some of the thoughts above. He says you have to be strong in yourself, so that your mind is no longer being taken over *by the thinker or pain-body*.[14] In doing so, he says, *you have made room for love, for joy, for peace*.[15] He concludes that when you reach this point, there are options. *You will then either separate—in love—or move ever more deeply into the Now together—into Being.*[16]

Eckhart Tolle is a complicated man. He presents the message of love, joy, and peace. It seems to be the same position that I present through Scripture, but he avoids consciously directing you to God—the Trinity: Father, Son, and Holy Spirit. He avoids mentioning Jesus' suffering, death, and resurrection. He is presenting partial truth. There are stern warnings in Scripture about partial truth, but I'm not here as judge. I know the man has a good heart.

Eckhart Tolle would want you to know the following statements. *What is God? The eternal One Life underneath all the forms of life. What is love? To feel the presence of that One Life deep within yourself and within all creatures. To be it. Therefore, all love is the love of God.*[17] In these statements is he clearly pointing to the Eternal God? Does he not have an underlying focus that you are God? His compass is a bit off course.

THIRD RECAPITULATION: Eckhart Tolle message is not complete. You will remember that on the back cover of his book he makes a point of stating that he *is a contemporary spiritual teacher who is not aligned with any particular religion or tradition*. Eckhart Tolle is taking truths, old ancient spiritual truths, and spinning them into his own mythology.

In reality, there is a Creator, God the Father, the I Am, who Loves you, His creation. The Father has a Son, Jesus, who, through the transforming action of His death and resurrection, made you righteous. The Son, through His sacrifice, gives you the right to enter into the Father's presence. From the Father and the Son, the Holy Spirit was given as a gift. The Holy Spirit leads you, through His flow, to experience the Glory of God's Love. This Glory shines through you and is attractive to humanity. Its purpose is to renew the earth. The brokenness of humanity and the world is transformed by your openness to the flow of the Rivers of Living Water.

The scriptural exegesis is quite simple, and gives understanding and meaning to your life. Your life is to be lived to the fullest on earth, flowing in the Holy Spirit and Love, glorifying the Creator, and preparing for eternity with Him.

RELATIONSHIPS AS SPIRITUAL PRACTICE

Eckhart Tolle in this section is writing about the plethora of broken and damaged relationships. There is also a discussion that dysfunctional relationships are negative and damaging to children. He goes on to state that there is an opportunity in the situations. *Why not cooperate with it instead of avoiding relationships or continuing to pursue the phantom of an ideal partner as an answer to your problems or a means of feeling fulfilled? The opportunity that is concealed within every crisis does not manifest until all the facts of any given situation are acknowledged and fully accepted.*[18] *With the acknowledgement and acceptance of the facts also comes a degree of freedom from them.*[19] What becomes clear is that you cannot heal yourself, nor can you fix your partner, but you can come to peace with the idea of knowing the flaws.

In reality, Eckhart Tolle is not giving you the Scriptural information about healing that is available. Let's look a little deeper into what Scripture would do with these thoughts.

First, you need to understand that in the union of a man and woman, the Creator forms a special bond. In the union you are spiritually united to your partner.

> [20] So the man gave names to all the livestock, the birds in the sky and all the wild animals. But for Adam no suitable helper was found. [21] So the LORD God caused the man to fall into a deep sleep; and while he was sleeping, he took one of the man's ribs and then closed up the place with flesh. [22] Then the LORD God made a woman from the rib he had

> taken out of the man, and he brought her to the man. ²³ The man said, "This is now bone of my bones and flesh of my flesh; she shall be called 'woman,' for she was taken out of man." ²⁴ That is why a man leaves his father and mother and is united to his wife, and they become one flesh.
> **Genesis 2: 20-24**

The Creator, Love, saw that Adam did not have a suitable helper. This shows that in the Creative Design, the relationship between a man and a woman was a significant part of the plan. *Bone of my bone and flesh of my flesh* emphasizes this close relationship: man and woman united in a union, with a deep level of connectivity and shared identity. Scripture then concludes that the two are joined together, separate from their families, and become one flesh.

'One flesh' is a Scriptural reference often referenced by this phrase, "When two come together, they become one," which typically describes the concept of marriage. Marriage is the union of a man and woman united to form a single, committed partnership.

Scripture goes on to express this more firmly by directions regarding divorce.

¹ When Jesus had finished saying these things, he left Galilee and went into the region of Judea to the other side of the Jordan. ² Large crowds followed him, and he healed them there. ³ Some Pharisees came to him to test him. They asked, "Is it lawful for a man to divorce his wife for any and every reason?" ⁴ "Haven't you read," he replied, "that at the beginning the Creator 'made them male and female,' ⁵ and said, 'For this reason a man will leave his father and mother and be united to his wife, and the two will become one flesh'? ⁶ So they are no longer two, but one flesh. Therefore what God has joined together, let no one separate."
Matthew 19: 1-6

In the Scripture, Jesus is asked whether or not it is lawful for a man to divorce his wife. He replies, do you not know that the Creator made them male and female? This again affirms the direction to join together in marriage and that it is Love's design. He goes on to repeat the words from Genesis, confirming again the message of the two becoming one flesh, not to be separated.

With these Scriptures, you see that Eckhart Tolle has not given you all the facts. It is clearly the Creator's design for a man and woman to marry, and it is the Creator's design that they stay together. Would your Creator design this and not give you the tools you need to stay together?

Healing is available. How is it available to you? It is through the spiritual bond, one flesh. You can think of one flesh as a spiritual bond that keeps you together through the thick and the thin, turmoil and troubles. That is why couples repeatedly come back together. Couples always feel drawn to each other, even in conflict. What Eckhart Tolle earlier calls a love/hate relationship.

'One flesh' is the invisible bond that occurs when a man and woman come together in sexual union. This is why you are directed, not to have sex outside of the bonds of marriage. How many times can you be one flesh? For those who have been sexually active, the question would be, to how many people are you bound? And added to this question might be, with these other one flesh bonds, can you have a positive, fulfilled relationship with your marital partner?

Eckhart Tolle suggests the opportunity for healing but does not give you the understanding when he says the following. *So whenever your relationship is not working, whenever it brings out the "madness" in you and your partner, be glad. What was unconscious is being brought up to the light. It is an opportunity for salvation.*[20]

The salvation comes because the Creator gives you the indwelling Holy Spirit. The Holy Spirit that is available to you offers you healing and gifts, manifestations of the word of knowledge, the word of wisdom, understanding, healing, and miracles (1 Corinthians 12). Through the use of these manifestations of the Holy Spirit, you as a couple, can work through any and all of the troubles of life.

Eckhart Tolle is asked, what should a person do when their partner is exhibiting negative behavior or behaving from their unconscious or ego? His response is good. *Instead of fighting the darkness, you bring in the light. Instead of reacting to delusion, you see the delusion yet at the same time look through it. Being the knowing creates a clear space of loving presence that allows all things and all people to be as they are. No greater catalyst for transformation exists. If you practice this, your partner cannot stay with you and remain unconscious.*[21] What is he saying in these statements? *Being the knowing* means being aware of the problem of your partner and not responding out of your own ego or unconscious, withholding judgement, and being able to control your reaction because you are at peace.

Scripture expresses the principle in this manner.

> [4] Love is patient, love is kind. It does not envy, it does not boast, it is not proud. [5] It does not dishonor others, it is not self-seeking, it is not easily angered, it keeps no record of wrongs. [6] Love does not delight in evil but rejoices with the truth. [7] It always protects, always trusts, always hopes, always perseveres. [8] Love never fails...
> 1 Corinthians 13: 4-8

Love never fails! Love is the catalyst. Love helps you to persevere. Eckhart Tolle is not giving a complete message when he directs that you should live out of your *loving presence*. Scripture would say, live out of the Love you have received as you abide in the vine. To abide is to dwell, to connect, and to remain within. It is a posture out of a place of proximity. By acting out of Love, you will not be drawn into your partner's problem, and your behavior will reflect your inner peace and beauty. *No greater catalyst for transformation exists.*[22] *If your partner is still identified with the mind and pain-body while you are already free, this will represent a major challenge—not to you but to your partner.*[23] Love never fails.

The encouragement in Eckhart Tolle's material is that change is possible. That your awareness of the negative in an issue; without joining the negative, gives you the opportunity to express your inner nature. Eckhart Tolle is saying that you are *accessing the power of the Now and initiating the transmutation of the pain.*[24] I would say you have accessed Love, whose source is God; that is the transmutation, the action of changing your state or position. In that position, connected to the source of Love, you are able to act out of Love.

Eckhart Tolle is close but not on target. You will note that a Scriptural view is quite a switch. It is a transmutation, a switch from acting in yourself, your power, your Now, to acting out of your inner nature, which is Love, derived from the source who is God and God is Love.

WHY WOMEN ARE CLOSER TO ENLIGHTENMENT

Generally speaking, Eckhart Tolle states, *it is easier for a woman to feel and be in her body, so she is naturally closer to Being and potentially closer to enlightenment than a man.*[25] On the other hand, he states *that the energy frequency of the mind appears to be essentially male.*[26] Eckhart Tolle contrasts the two positions, male and female, by stating, *To go beyond the mind and reconnect with a deeper reality of Being, very different qualities are needed: surrender, nonjudgment, openness that allows life to be instead of resisting it, the capacity to hold all things in the loving embrace of your knowing. All these qualities are much more closely related to the female principle.*[27]

Eckhart Tolle points out that, *as a general rule, the major obstacle for men tends to be the thinking mind, and the major obstacle for women the pain-body...*[28]

When you think of these statements, you are reminded that Love is described in Scripture as having both male and female characteristics.

> ¹⁵ "Can a mother forget the baby at her breast and have no compassion on the child she has borne? Though she may forget, I will not forget you!
> Isaiah 49: 15

Love's nature is both nurturing and protecting, like the mother who has the baby at her breast.

> ¹² For this is what the LORD says: "I will extend peace to her like a river, and the wealth of nations like a flooding stream; you will nurse and be carried on her arm and dandled on her knees. ¹³ As a mother comforts her child, so will I comfort you; and you will be comforted over Jerusalem."
> Isaiah 66: 12-13

Love is imaged as nursing, cuddling, and comforting. These are true, but the more common reference to God in Scripture contrasts these with the masculine, where He is Creator—omnipotent, omniscient, and omnipresent.

In reality, Eckhart Tolle's position does not provide the complete picture of God. Let me remind you of Genesis, where you were created in God's image. Both men and women were created in God's image.

> ²⁷ So God created mankind in his own image, in the image of God he created them; male and female he created them.
> Genesis 1: 27

'God transcends the human distinction between the sexes. He is neither man nor woman; He is God.' ²⁹

DISSOLVING THE COLLECTIVE FEMALE PAIN-BODY

A question asked of Eckhart Tolle: *Why is the pain-body more of an obstacle for women?* ³⁰ To explain this, Eckhart Tolle states *The pain-body usually has a collective as well as personal aspect.*³¹ What he states is that you have personal pain, but you also accumulate the pain from the collective human race. He gives an example of the *accumulated pain suffered by women partially through male subjugation of the female, through slavery, exploitation, rape, childbirth, child loss, and so on, of the thousands of years.*³² He suggests that women are often taken over by this pain-body. That *it has an extremely powerful energetic charge that can easily pull you into unconscious identification with it.*³³

Eckhart Tolle goes on to explain that this energy can drive you and that you could feed on it. His instruction is, *your main task as a woman now is to transmute the pain-body so that it no longer comes between you and your true self, the essence of who you are.*[34] What Eckhart Tolle is talking about, *to transmute*, is what I call Inner Healing Prayer. Through Inner Healing Prayer you can transmute and change both the form and nature of the pain-body through the exchange at the Cross of Jesus. On the Cross, Jesus took on your pain, sin, and human brokenness, exchanging it for the blessings due to Him.

(Learn about the Exchange at the Cross by reading Appendix B.)

Once again, I refer you to my book, *Five Fold Cycle – Method of Healing Personal Hurt,* where you can learn to apply the five steps in Inner Healing.

GIVE UP THE RELATIONSHIP WITH YOURSELF

In this section Eckhart Tolle is answering the question, *would one still have a need for a relationship* if you were whole and fully conscious?[35] His response is, *Enlightened or not, you are either a man or a woman, so on level of your form identity you are not complete. You are one-half of the whole. This incompleteness is felt as a male-female attraction, the pull toward the opposite energy polarity, no matter how conscious you are.*[36] What you can understand from this is that there is always a pull for a man to join a woman, or a woman to join a man.

You can understand this attraction based on creation and the direction from the Creator described in Matthew.

> [4] "Haven't you read," he replied, "that at the beginning the Creator 'made them male and female,' [5] and said, 'For this reason a man will leave his father and mother and be united to his wife, and the two will become one flesh'? [6] So they are no longer two, but one flesh...
> Matthew 19: 4-6

Made male and female, the two come together to become one, the natural *opposite energy* attraction.

Next, Eckhart Tolle answers the question: *Is being gay a help or hindrance, or does it not make any difference?* [37] He explains that it may give you some advantage because you are outside of the norm, but at the same time *you will play roles and games dictated by a mental image you have of yourself as gay. You will become unconscious. You will become unreal. Under your ego mask, you will become very unhappy.*[38] I suggest that you look into this topic through my first book, *Five Fold Cycle – Method Of Healing Personal Hurt.* There is a section called *What About Sexual Issues,* which presents a story about Jim, who started to wonder about his homosexual identity. In that section of the book, you will gain some idea of how to receive healing by searching into your homosexual roots.

(Learn about the *Five Fold Cycle – Method of Healing Personal Hurt* by reading Appendix C.)

This question was posed to Eckhart Tolle, *is it not true that you need to have a good relationship with yourself and love yourself before you can have a fulfilling relationship with another person?* [39] Once again, Eckhart Tolle, in his excessive chatter and garrulity, discusses that the person has split themselves in two, a subject and an object, a mind-created duality.[40]

His complexity and confusing ideas do not help. Scripture gives a simpler and more complete answer to the question.

> ^{37} Jesus replied: 'Love the Lord your God with all your heart and with all your soul and with all your mind.' ^{38} This is the first and greatest commandment. ^{39} And the second is like it: 'Love your neighbor as yourself.'
> Matthew 22: 37-39

You are to Love God first. Remember that God is the source of Love, and from His love comes your Being and your Love. Next, you are to Love your neighbor as yourself. A good gauge of whether or not you love your neighbor as you love yourself would be your application of this Scripture.

> ^{3} Do nothing out of selfish ambition or vain conceit. Rather, in humility value others above yourselves, ^{4} not looking to your own interests but each of you to the interests of the others.
> Philippians 2: 3-4

The application would be doing nothing out of selfish ambition or vain conceit. You are to work out of humility, keeping your interest in others. Matthew and Philippians provide a biblical context, often interpreted as prioritizing others and placing God's will over personal desires. The emphasis is on being humble and loving others as oneself.

In the end, all your relationships are to be based in Love, the Love derived from the source of Love.

CHAPTER NINE
BEYOND HAPPINESS AND UNHAPPINESS THERE IS PEACE

THE HIGHER GOOD BEYOND GOOD AND BAD

In this section Eckhart Tolle responds to questions about positive and negative things happening in people's lives and the fact that you cannot control life's situations. He also reflects on the difference between happiness and inner peace.

He makes a statement: *Seen from a higher perspective, conditions are always positive. To be more precise: they are neither positive nor negative.*[1] He goes on to say that when you accept this fact, *there is no good or bad in your life anymore.*[2]

This idea is explained in the Scripture to the Romans.

> [28] And we know that in all things God works for the good of those who love him, who have been called according to his purpose.
> Romans 8: 28

When you are connected to Love, the Love relationship, Love will use all things for your good. *All things* mean every incident in your life, whether one might see them as negative or positive, good or bad. Through Scripture you gain a more complete understanding of Eckhart Tolle's message. He would not make this statement, but the fact is the higher perspective, higher good, is experienced when you are connected to Love.

Eckhart Tolle wants you to relax and realize that things are the way they are, that your 'presence' gives you the strength to endure. In reality, he is leaving out the fact that it isn't your strength, it is the strength you receive from God, who is Love.

Another question is posed to Eckhart Tolle. *This sounds to me like denial and Self-deception.*[3] He replies, *You're not pretending anything. You are allowing it to be as it is, that's all.*[4] In reality, Eckhart Tolle is missing out on the fullness of Scripture. To be able to relax and let things be as they are, you need the Fruit of the Spirit: peace, patience, gentleness, etc.

A third comment in this section refers back to forgiveness. *Forgiveness of the present is even more important than forgiveness of the past. If you forgive every moment—allow it to be as it is—then there will be no accumulation of resentment that needs to be forgiven at some later time.*[5] Eckhart Tolle is giving you the gist of the idea of forgiveness and its effects, but Scripture gives you the complete message.

> [14] For if you forgive other people when they sin against you, your heavenly Father will also forgive you. [15] But if you do not forgive others their sins, your Father will not forgive your sins.
> Matthew 6: 14-15

The sin of unforgiveness is a barrier in your relationship to Love. Unforgiveness inhibits you from receiving Love's blessings and gifts. Sin only disappears when you bring them to Jesus on the Cross. You are to apply Jesus' blood sacrifice on the Cross and apprehend His blessings. When this is done, the legal issue that has limited you is removed. Scripture would say the devil has no more legal right. The removal of the barrier allows blessings and healing to flow.

> [10] your kingdom come, your will be done, on earth as it is in heaven. [11] Give us today our daily bread. [12] And forgive us our debts, as we also have forgiven our debtors. [13] And lead us not into temptation, but deliver us from the evil one.
> Matthew 6: 10-13

The Scripture from Matthew, known as the Our Father, emphasizes the underlying equation. You are challenged by God/Love to forgive your debtors, those who hurt you. Unforgiveness opens you to temptation by the evil one. By forgiving, you are no longer under the threat of the evil one, because you are now reconnected to Love and Love's protection.

FOURTH RECAPITULATION:
The summation is, if you are connected to Love, you will have that inner peace that passes all understanding. Situations will come and go, both positive and negative, good or bad, but as you release them, as you forgive, you remain in that peace, because you are connected to Love. Peace is not based on the situation or the feeling of happiness but rather the spiritual connection with Love. Eckhart Tolle describes it in this manner: *there may be sadness and tears, but provided that you have relinquished resistance, underneath the sadness you will feel a deep serenity, the stillness, a sacred presence. This is the emanation of Being, this is inner peace, the good that has no opposite.*[6]

You accept what is because you know that Love has His hand on you.

> [13] Your kingdom is an everlasting kingdom, and your dominion endures through all generations. The LORD is trustworthy in all he promises and faithful in all he does. [14] The LORD upholds all who fall and lifts up all who are bowed down. [15] The eyes of all look to you, and you give them their food at the proper time. [16] You open your hand and satisfy the desires of every living thing. [17] The LORD is righteous in all his ways and faithful in all he does. [18] The LORD is near to all who call on him, to all who call on him in truth. [19] He fulfills the desires of those who fear him; he hears their cry and saves them. [20] The LORD watches over all who love him, but all the wicked he will destroy.
> **Psalm 145: 13-20**

You can be sure, that all things work unto good for those who are connected to Love. Love is trustworthy. Love upholds all who fail and lifts them up. Love will provide for you and satisfy your desires. Love is righteous and true. Love hears your cries, fulfills your desires, and watches over you; not so the wicked, who are outside of His Love and protection.

(Learn about The Art of Forgiveness by reading Appendix E.)

THE END OF YOUR LIFE DRAMA

What are life's dramas to Eckhart Tolle? *Most of the so-called bad things that happened in people's lives are due to unconsciousness. They are self-created, or rather ego-created,*[7] he states. If I were to translate this, it means that you have not cleaned up the historical issues in your life and that you are focusing on the troubles of today; therefore, you cannot act in power and presence, the Now as he calls it. Eckhart Tolle calls this drama. He goes on to say, *when you're fully conscious, drama does not come into your life anymore.*[8] He makes a number of other statements to complete this thought. *When you live in complete acceptance of what is, that is the end of all drama in your life. No one can even have an argument with you, no matter how hard he or she tries.*[9] *You can still make your point clearly and firmly, but there will be no reactive force behind it, no defense or attack.*[10] Although Eckhart Tolle does not direct you to God in these matters, these statements give a good image of what it means to be fully united, fully connected, and one with Love; one with God: Father, Son, and Holy Spirit.

Love becomes the Center. To be at the 'center' means being the midpoint, the most important or pivotal point, or the source and center of your heart.

You can judge whether or not your life reflects Love by asking three questions:

- Am I living my life as a response to God's grace and Love?
- Am I living my life serving my neighbor with Love?
- Am I a reflection of Love?

IMPERMANENCE AND THE CYCLES OF LIFE

I enjoy Eckhart Tolle's philosophic messages. In this chapter, however, he seems to have relinquished his power position and is somewhat reluctantly succumbing to life. He describes the impermanence of life and the changing cycles.

On the level of form, there is birth and death, creation and destruction, growth and dissolution, of seemingly separate forms.

This is reflected everywhere: in the life cycle of a star or a planet, a physical body, a tree, a flower; in the rise and fall of nations, political systems, civilizations; and in the inevitable cycles of gain and loss in the life of an individual.[11] He goes on to say that there are down cycles and up cycles; there are cycles of good and cycles that are not good. *If you cling and resist at any point, it means you are refusing to go with the flow of life, and you will suffer.*[12]

Eckhart Tolle gets to the point here. Scripture from Ecclesiastes will give you more depth—there is a time for everything under heaven.

> [1] There is a time for everything, and a season for every activity under the heavens: [2] a time to be born and a time to die, a time to plant and a time to uproot, [3] a time to kill and a time to heal, a time to tear down and a time to build, [4] a time to weep and a time to laugh, a time to mourn and a time to dance, [5] a time to scatter stones and a time to gather them, a time to embrace and a time to refrain from embracing, [6] a time to search and a time to give up, a time to keep and a time to throw away, [7] a time to tear and a time to mend, a time to be silent and a time to speak, [8] a time to

love and a time to hate, a time for war and a time for peace. ⁹ What do workers gain from their toil? ¹⁰ I have seen the burden God has laid on the human race. ¹¹ He has made everything beautiful in its time. He has also set eternity in the human heart; yet no one can fathom what God has done from beginning to end. ¹² I know that there is nothing better for people than to be happy and to do good while they live. ¹³ That each of them may eat and drink, and find satisfaction in all their toil—this is the gift of God.
Ecclesiastes 3: 1-13

Scripture develops Eckhart Tolle's idea and gives it fullness; there is a time for everything. The clarity comes at the end of Ecclesiastes; starting at verse 9, even in your toil, God has made everything beautiful in its time. He has set eternity in your heart, even though you can't grasp eternity's infinite wonder. As you live in Love and Love's presence lives in you, you will experience the gift of God—Love. Isn't Scripture amazing!

Later in this section Eckhart Tolle says you should not look for your identity in life's events—happiness, success, suffering, or dis-satisfaction—*But to seek something through them that they cannot give—an identity, the sense of permanency and fulfillment—is a recipe for frustration and suffering.*[13]

He goes on to say, *Many people never realize that there can be no "salvation" in anything they do, possess, or attain. Those who do realize it often become world-weary and depressed: If nothing can give you the true fulfillment, what is there left to strive for, what is the point in anything?*[14] These statements offer a very depressing view. Eckhart Tolle then refers to the Old Testament prophecy about vanity. Scripture, you will see, provide a more complete and satisfying message.

> [1] The words of the Preacher, the son of David, king in Jerusalem. [2] Vanity of vanities, saith the Preacher, vanity of vanities; all is vanity. [3] What profit hath a man of all his labour which he taketh under the sun? [4] One generation passeth away, and another generation cometh: but the earth abideth for ever. [5] The sun also ariseth, and the sun goeth down, and hasteth to his place where he arose. [6] The wind goeth toward the south, and turneth about unto the north; it whirleth about continually, and the wind returneth again according to

> his circuits. ⁷ All the rivers run into the sea; yet the sea is not full; unto the place from whence the rivers come, thither they return again. ⁸ All things are full of labour; man cannot utter it: the eye is not satisfied with seeing, nor the ear filled with hearing.
> **Ecclesiastes 1: 1-8 KJV**

Yes, Scripture agrees with Eckhart Tolle that everything is vanity. The upside, however, is found in this Scripture—deep calls to deep.

> ⁷ Deep calls to deep in the roar of your waterfalls; all your waves and breakers have swept over me. ⁸ By day the LORD directs his love, at night his song is with me—a prayer to the God of my life.
> **Psalm 42: 7-8**

Your identity is not to be found in what you do, what happens to you, nor the events of life. Your identity is to be found deep within the deep roar of the flowing waters, Rivers of Living Water. Through this deep place within your body, the temple of Christ, you will be led by Love. Even in times of sleep, Love's song is with you; its frequency connects you.

USING AND RELINQUISHING NEGATIVITY

Negativity ranges from irritation or impatience to fierce anger, from a depressed mood or sullen resentment to suicidal despair. Sometimes the resistance triggers the emotional pain-body, in which case even a minor situation may produce intense negativity, such as anger, depression, or deep grief.[15] In these statements, Eckhart Tolle is setting the stage for you to understand how you should release negativity. He emphasizes this idea with this statement. *Negativity is totally unnatural. It is a psychic pollutant, and there is a deep link between the poisoning and destruction of nature and the vast negativity that has accumulated in the collective human psyche. No other life-form on the planet knows negativity, only humans, just as no other life-form violates and poisons the Earth that sustains it.*[16]

In this section, he is comparing humanity's flawed negativity to the beauty of nature. A flower is never unhappy. The dolphin is never depressed. He states that only animals in close proximity to humans ever express *negativity or show signs of neurotic behavior.*[17]

I am reminded of Saint Francis of Assisi, who is renowned as the patron saint of animals, often depicted surrounded by creatures, particularly birds and a wolf, who were purported to come to him to listen to his sermon.

Eckhart Tolle is telling people to catch these moments—these negative thoughts and inspirations. He directs that you should *look on it as a voice saying "Attention. Here and Now. Wake up."*[18] Scripture gives a very good teaching on how to handle everything that runs through your mind.

You will remember Romans 12: 2:

> *[2] Do not conform to the pattern of this world, but be transformed by the renewing of your mind. Then you will be able to test and approve what God's will is—his good, pleasing and perfect will.*
> **Romans 12: 2**

It teaches about transformation and transcendence. Transcendence is going beyond the material and the natural to the supernatural driven by Love. Transformation is metanoia, a call to 'change one's mind' or undergo a deep transformation in perspective and way of life.

You can reach this plateau by refocusing your mind and heart as expressed in the Scripture from Philippians 4: 6-9, which instructed that you should refocus, petitioning Love with a thankful heart. You focus on whatever is pure, lovely, admirable, excellent, and praiseworthy. As you practice this refocusing, the negativity slips away, you open to the peace that transcends all understanding, and healing occurs.

THE NATURE OF COMPASSION

Eckhart Tolle presents a wonderful image of how you can be at peace, like the body of a lake, yet the surface is being ruffled by the wind and the business of life.

Having gone beyond the mind-made opposites, you become like a deep lake. The outer situation of your life and whatever happens there is the surface of the lake. Sometimes calm, sometimes windy and rough, according to the cycles and seasons. Deep down, however, the lake is always undisturbed.[19] He explains that in this state you are not ruffled by situations around you because you have found your own inner strength—you are at peace.

Compassion, then, *is the awareness of the deep bond between yourself and all creatures,*[20] with the same fragile bodies and vulnerability, that ends in mortality. He is suggesting that you meditate on your mortality, quoting the phrase *Die before you die.*[21] What does all this mean?

Scripture gives you two teachings that bring understanding to Eckhart Tolle's message. Revelation 21 gives an understanding that there is death, but following death you will be in Love's presence.

> [4] *'He will wipe every tear from their eyes. There will be no more death' or mourning or crying or pain, for the old order of things has passed away.* Revelation 21: 4

There will be no tears, as Love will wipe away your tears. There will be no more death, mourning, crying, or pain; the old will be gone, and the new will be present.

Jesus' Love will comfort you.

> [1] *"Do not let your hearts be troubled. You believe in God; believe also in me.* [2] *My Father's house has many rooms; if that were not so, would I have told you that I am going there to prepare a place for you?* [3] *And if I go and prepare a place*

> for you, I will come back and take you to be with me that you also may be where I am. ⁴ You know the way to the place where I am going."
> John 14: 1-4

You are to take comfort; the Father has provided a place for you. You are to be assured that the Son, Jesus, will come back and take you to be with Him. Scripture implies that deep within, as *deep calls to deep*, you know this place that is centered inside you. These are clear references to the indwelling of the Holy Spirit and the unity that you have through the Holy Spirit.

TOWARD A DIFFERENT ORDER OF REALITY

In this section there is a discussion posing the question, does your body need to die? Scripture explains this quite simply.

> ²³ *For the wages of sin is death, but the gift of God is eternal life in Christ Jesus our Lord.*
> Romans 6: 23

Scripture explains that God had warned Adam; death is the consequence of sin, a penalty for Adam's disobedience. Death then became a natural part of the human experience, with the promise of eternal life in Christ for those who believe.

Another person questioned Eckhart Tolle saying, *I don't agree the body needs to die. I am convinced that we can achieve physical immortality. We believe in death and that's why the body dies.*[22] This question isn't far off, although Eckhart Tolle goes off on a tangent about the illusion of the body and of death.

In Scripture, there were a few people who did not face physical death; Enoch and Elijah are two examples.

> [5] By faith Enoch was taken from this life, so that he did not experience death: "He could not be found, because God had taken him away." For before he was taken, he was commended as one who pleased God.
> **Hebrews 11: 5**
>
> [11] As they were walking along and talking together, suddenly a chariot of fire and horses of fire appeared and separated the two of them, and Elijah went up to heaven in a whirlwind.
> **2 Kings 2: 11**

What made the difference in the lives of these two men that they did not physically die? Enoch was commended as one who pleased God. Elijah was removed from Earth with a chariot and horse of fire. Where he goes is not conclusive, but the fact that he left bodily was witnessed by a party of 50 men. Scripture describes Elijah as a powerful and courageous prophet and righteous man, known for his unwavering faith, boldness in confronting evil, and ability to perform miracles, including bringing fire from heaven and calling down a drought.

These two men of the Old Testament reached a position, a connection with God, that allowed them to circumvent death. They experienced a different order of reality. This different order of reality becomes a target for all of humanity, including you.

To summarize Eckhart Tolle, you might say it is only when you reach the roots of the Unmanifested, this deep relationship with Love, *no longer bound to this world, this level of reality,*[23] that you are in a position where you can transcend. *It is only at this point that you are able to feel true compassion and to help others...*[24] Eckhart Tolle concludes that *only those who have transcended the world can bring about a better world.*[25]

Scripture describes how this presence emanates from you, because you become both salt and light.

> [13] "You are the salt of the earth. But if the salt loses its saltiness, how can it be made salty again? It is no longer good for anything, except to be thrown out and trampled underfoot. [14] "You are the light of the world. A town built on a hill cannot be hidden. [15] Neither do people light a lamp and put it under a bowl. Instead they put it on its stand, and it gives light to everyone in the house. [16] In the same way, let your light shine before others, that they may see your good deeds and glorify your Father in heaven.
> Matthew 5: 13-16

You are to become salt and light to the world around you. These qualities are the flavor and energy emission that nourishes and brightens the world and encourages others. This is the difference that comes with Love's reality and the nature of Loving compassion.

FIFTH RECAPITULATION:
You are encouraged to leave drama behind and be centered. Being centered means to be

fully united, fully connected, and one with Love. One with God: Father, Son, and Holy Spirit. Love becomes the Center. You are invited into a relationship in which you will grow.

There is an impermanence with life, and there are changing cycles, both positive and negative, good or bad. In all of this you are to forgive and remain in peace by connecting to Love. Peace is not based on the situation or the feeling of happiness, but rather on the spiritual connection with Love.

There is a time for everything, and a season for every activity under the heavens. God has made everything beautiful in its time. He has set eternity in your heart. As you live in Love and Love's presence lives in you, you will experience the fullness of the gift—Love.

You are to relinquish negative thoughts and inspirations; be transformed by the renewing of your mind. This transformation comes with being led by the Holy Spirit, being attached like a branch to the vine. Through this relationship you gain *The Nature Of Compassion*, a title used a few pages back, and form a new reality—ordered, pure, peaceful, and loving. Scripture would refer to this as the New Life.

You stand strong, being light and salt, standing on the rock-solid foundation of Love, assured that Love will take you home.

It's all about Love

CHAPTER TEN
THE MEANING OF SURRENDER

ACCEPTANCE OF THE NOW

As I have said before, I enjoy Eckhart Tolle. He is a good man. In this section, *Acceptance Of The Now*, Eckhart Tolle presents a very good idea. I would like to flesh it out a bit for you by providing the depth of Scripture. First, look at the question that is posed and his response.

You mentioned "surrender" a few times. I don't like the idea. It sounds somewhat fatalistic. If we always accept the way things are, we're not going to make any effort to improve them. It seems to me what progress is all about, both in our personal lives and collectively, is not to accept the limitations of the present but to strive to go beyond them and create something better. If we hadn't done this, we would still be living in caves. How do you reconcile surrender with changing things and getting things done?[1]

How do you reconcile surrender with changing things and getting things done? Eckhart Tolle answers, *To some people, surrender may have negative connotations, implying defeat, giving up, failing to rise to the challenge of life, becoming lethargic, and so on. True surrender, however, is something entirely different. It does not mean to passively put up with whatever situation you find yourself in and to do nothing about it. Nor does it mean to cease making plans or initiating positive action. Surrender is the simple but profound wisdom of 'yielding to' rather than 'opposing' the flow of life.*[2] Eckhart Tolle answers well but of course there is more to the message.

How do you express this in Scripture? In Scripture, surrender means listening for and following the lead of the Holy Spirit, that little voice inside that is the voice of God's indwelling Holy Spirit. Jeremiah provides an understanding of how this works.

The message from Jeremiah is to God's people who are in exile in Egypt because they failed to listen to the Lord.

> [11] For I know the plans I have for you," declares the LORD, "plans to prosper you and not to harm you, plans to give you hope and a future. [12] Then you will call on me and come and pray to me, and I will listen to you. [13] You will seek me and find me when you seek me with all your heart. [14] I will be found by you," declares the LORD, "and will bring

you back from captivity.[a] I will gather you from all the nations and places where I have banished you," declares the LORD, "and will bring you back to the place from which I carried you into exile."
Jeremiah 29: 11-14
Footnotes
a. *will restore your fortunes*

For I know the plans I have for you. **There is a plan, a path, available to you to prosper. There is hope for the future.** You are encouraged to choose, to pray, call on Love with all your heart. The heart, as you will see in the next Scripture, is an important center in your Being. With the call from your heart, you will find what you are seeking. You will be gathered up and brought back to union with the source of Love—your fortunes will be restored. Fortunes mean more than money; they mean the necessities to keep you in Love's essence.

Your heart is important.

> [20] My son, pay attention to what I say; turn your ear to my words. [21] Do not let them out of your sight, keep them within your heart; [22] for they are life to those who find them and health to one's whole body. [23] Above

> all else, guard your heart, for everything you do flows from it.
> Proverbs 4: 20-23

Everything flows from your heart. You will remember the Rivers of Living Water, the Holy Spirit indwelling in your gut, sometimes referred to as your heart. The heart is the wellspring of your body. It is from the heart that life springs. You are to tune your attention, hearing, sight, and heart to the lead of the Holy Spirit, who will give life. These four modalities—attention, hearing, sight, and heart—assures *life to those who find them and health to one's whole body.* It is a wonderful message of Scripture! You are promised life, its vigor and vitality; as well as health to your whole body, including mind, body, soul, and spirit.

As I summed up the last section, I thought, "Eckhart Tolle's message would be on the right path if he would provide you the full benefits of Scripture."

He goes on in this section, to refer to a line in Scripture from Jesus—"*the one thing is needed.*"[3] The line is taken from a reference in Scripture to Martha and Mary, whom Jesus was visiting.

[41] "Martha, Martha," the Lord answered, "you are worried and upset about many things, [42] but few things are needed—or indeed only one.[a] Mary has chosen what is better, and it will not be taken away from her."
Luke 10: 41-42
Footnotes
a. *but only one thing is needed*

Mary sat at the feet of Jesus and listened to His teaching. Martha was busy getting things ready, fussing about the domestic matters that would be needed. Martha returned and complained about her sister Mary not helping. Jesus responded, *"the one thing that is needed."* That one thing was to be attentive to Jesus and His teaching. You know from previous Scriptures that if you are attentive to Love, Love will take care of you.

Acceptance of the Now is in reality, an openness to being led by the indwelling Holy Spirit. You use the four modalities: attention, hearing, sight, and heart. Your openness is the one thing that will drive your heart and give life to those who find them and health to one's whole body. Surrender means being open to the Holy Spirit's lead.

FROM MIND ENERGY TO SPIRITUAL ENERGY

The question was posed: *letting go of resistance is easier said than done.*[4] Eckhart Tolle presents the idea that *if you're conscious, that is to say totally present in the Now, all negativity would dissolve almost instantly. It could not survive in your presence.*[5] This portion of Eckhart Tolle's message is good. In my book, *Five Fold Cycle Workbook,*[6] I presented a 'Spiritual Law—What You Focus On is What You Get.' Scripture has presented the idea that when you focus on your problems, they begin to cloud you; on the other hand, Scripture has directed you to look away from your problems and focus on things of Love.

> [8] Finally, brothers and sisters, whatever is true, whatever is noble, whatever is right, whatever is pure, whatever is lovely, whatever is admirable—if anything is excellent or praiseworthy—think about such things.
> Philippians 4: 8

What you focus on is what you get. Whatever you give your attention to, whatever you feed, is what grows and develops in your heart and mind. The more you grasp the essence of Scripture, the more you come to realize that everything depends upon the attitude of your will. Do you join with Love—*Thy Kingdom come*? Do you seek to be led by the Holy Spirit—*Thy will be done*? In the prayer, you are joining like a branch to the vine, opening your personal will to the will of Love—God is Love. Love never transgresses a person's will; rather, Love shows the path to wholeness and freedom and opens the mind to your inheritance as Love's children.

You are reminded of the old Cherokee story of the Two Wolves—Be Careful Which Wolf You Feed.

The old Cherokee was speaking to his grandson about a battle that goes on inside people. The battle is between the good wolf and the bad wolf.

The grandson posed a question: "Which wolf wins?"

The old Cherokee replied, "The one you feed."

This is such deep wisdom, put so simply and beautifully. Everyone, like yourself, has parts of good, bad, and ugly within them, but it depends solely on which attitudes you wish should dominate your moods or outlook. You can choose to brood and drown in self-pity instead of looking at the brighter side of the situation you find yourself in. You are to find a way out of it with a positive attitude. It is all a matter of choices, 'your' choices. You have control over those choices. Aptly said, be careful which wolf you feed.

SURRENDER IN PERSONAL RELATIONSHIPS

Interpersonal relationships always add a dynamic. Eckhart Tolle gives a very good explanation of how to approach the difficult situations. *If you resist or fight unconscious behavior in others, you become unconscious yourself. But surrender doesn't mean that you allow yourself to be used by unconscious people. Not at all. It is perfectly possible to say "no" firmly and clearly to a person or to walk away from a situation and be in the state of complete inner nonresistance at the same time. When you say "no" to a person or situation, let it come not from reaction but from insight, from a clear realization of what is right or not right for you at that moment.*[7]

What he clearly presents is the old adage, let your no be no, and your yes be yes. The idea is found in Scripture where it instructs you not to swear oaths.

> [37] All you need to say is simply 'Yes' or 'No'; anything beyond this comes from the evil one.[a]
> Matthew 5: 37
> Footnotes
> a. *from evil*

When you are secure in the peace within and not working from your pain-body, woundedness, or hurt, you are able to access that power of the Holy Spirit from within and stand secure. In this security, you speak without your words being colored by anger, hurt, or other negative; people's reactions are muted because they do not feel attacked. They will sense from you a maturity and Love.

There was another question presented: *what about nonresistance in the face of violence, aggression, and the like?* [8] Once again Eckhart Tolle gives a very good answer. *Nonresistance doesn't necessarily mean doing nothing. All it means is that any "doing" becomes nonreactive. Remember the deep wisdom underlying the practice of Eastern martial arts: Don't resist the opponent's force. Yield to overcome.*[9]

TRANSFORMING ILLNESS INTO ENLIGHTENMENT

Eckhart Tolle presents two very good messages in this section. The first has to do with labeling, applying a negative label to yourself. An example might be "my arthritis," "my bad back," or "my diabetes." In making statements like that, you are accepting and agreeing to the sickness or illness in your body. Such conclusions or vows limit the potential for change. Eckhart Tolle states, *as you know, underneath the various conditions that make up your life situation, which exists in time, there is something deeper, more essential: your Life, your very Being in a timeless Now. As there are no problems in the Now, there is no illness either. The belief in a label that someone attaches to your condition keeps the condition in place, empowers it, and makes a seemingly solid reality out of a temporary imbalance.*[10]

If you would frame this in a Scriptural perspective, you might consider verses from Matthew 7, referring to ask, seek, and knock.

> [7] "Ask and it will be given to you; seek and you will find; knock and the door will be opened to you. [8] For everyone who asks receives; the one who seeks finds; and to the one who knocks, the door will be opened.
> Matthew 7: 7-8

In the Scripture from Matthew, Jesus stated, if you ask, it will be given to you; if you seek, you will find; and if you knock, the door will be opened. The corollary is, if you do not ask, you will not receive, if you do not seek, you will not find; and if you do not knock, the door will not be answered. Asking, seeking, and knocking are all acts of opening and expectation. None of these are possible if you have accepted your condition and labeled yourself. In this manner illness can be transformed, healing is a potential.

Eckhart Tolle's next message is also very good. *If you have a major illness, use it for enlightenment. Anything 'bad' that happens in your life—use it for enlightenment.*[11]

My old business card used to have a poem on the back, titled 'The Weaver.' This poem gives an image to Eckhart Tolle's message of how illness transforms.

THE WEAVER

My life is but a weaving
Between my Lord and me.
I cannot choose the colors
He worketh steadily.

Of times he weaveth sorrow,
And I in foolish pride
Forget He sees the upper
And I, the underside.

Not until the loom is silent
And the shuttles cease to fly
Shall God unroll the canvas
And explain the reason why.

The dark threads are as needful
In the Weaver's skillful hand
As the threads of
gold and silver
In the pattern He has planned.

He knows, He loves, He cares;
Nothing this truth can dim.
He gives the very best to those
Who leave the choice to Him.

-Author Unknown

WHEN DISASTER STRIKES

Once again Eckhart Tolle presents a message close to the truth. It's a repeat of the message from 'The Weaver.' *So whenever any kind of disaster strikes, or something goes seriously "wrong"—illness, disability, loss of home or fortune or of a socially defined identity, breakup of a close relationship, death or suffering of a loved one, or your own impending death—know that there is another side to it, that you are just one step away from something incredible: a complete alchemical transmutation of the base metal of pain and suffering into gold. That one step is called surrender.*[12]

Although Eckhart Tolle is close to the truth, you need to look further into Scripture. You are reminded that I suggest that transmutation comes through accessing Love, whose source is God.

⁷ But we have this treasure in jars of clay to show that this all-surpassing power is from God and not from us. ⁸ We are hard pressed on every side, but not crushed; perplexed, but not in despair; ⁹ persecuted, but not abandoned; struck down, but not destroyed. ¹⁰ We always carry around in our body the death of Jesus, so that the life of Jesus may also be revealed in our body. ¹¹ For we who are alive are always being given over to death for Jesus' sake, so that his life may also be revealed in our mortal body. ¹² So then, death is at work in us, but life is at work in you. ¹³ It is written: "I believed; therefore I have spoken." Since we have that same spirit of faith, we also believe and therefore speak, ¹⁴ because we know that the one who raised the Lord Jesus from the dead will also raise us with Jesus and present us with you to himself. ¹⁵ All this is for your benefit, so that the grace that is reaching more and more people may cause thanksgiving to overflow to the glory of God. ¹⁶ Therefore we do not lose heart. Though outwardly we are wasting away, yet inwardly we are being renewed day by day. ¹⁷ For our light and

momentary troubles are achieving for us an eternal glory that far outweighs them all. ⁱ⁸ So we fix our eyes not on what is seen, but on what is unseen, since what is seen is temporary, but what is unseen is eternal.
2 Corinthians 4: 7-18

You are a treasure in a jar of clay, which shows the *all-surpassing* power of Love. Suffering and death will indeed come, but grace and power overcome every trial and help you achieve your purpose and your essence. The indwelling Holy Spirit presence in you will draw more and more people and overflow into thanksgiving. Therefore we do not lose heart. Fix your eyes not on what is seen, but on what is unseen. Focus on the eternal.

You are to have an Eternal perspective.

TRANSFORMING SUFFERING INTO PEACE
In *Transforming Suffering Into Peace*, Eckhart Tolle refers back to surrender; you

are *to surrender each moment to the reality of the moment. Knowing that what is cannot be undone—because it already is—you say yes to what is or accept what isn't. Then you do what you have to do, whatever the situation requires. If you abide in this state of acceptance, you create no more negativity, no more suffering, no more unhappiness. You then live in a state of nonresistance, a state of grace and lightness, free of struggle.*[13] He goes on to explain that if you don't find that experience at the first chance of surrender, you always have another opportunity.

Eckhart Tolle's positive response also leads to a second statement equally good. *Do you want an easy death? Would you rather die without pain, without agony? Then die to the past every moment, and let the light of your presence shine away the heavy, time-bound self you thought of as "you."*[14] What did he mean by those statements? He is speaking about focus and presence.

As you will see, Scripture gives clarity and depth. When you focus on the eternal and let Love's grace heal the past, your light comes through. You experience Love's presence— you are one with the vine. Your identity comes not from yourself, but your identity comes from your relationship with the One who Loves you.

Scripture has many times referred to that transformation of suffering into peace.

> [51] Listen, I tell you a mystery: We will not all sleep, but we will all be changed— [52] in a flash, in the twinkling of an eye, at the last trumpet. For the trumpet will sound, the dead will be raised imperishable, and we will be changed. [53] For the perishable, must clothe itself with the imperishable, and the mortal with immortality. [54] When the perishable has been clothed with the imperishable, and the mortal with immortality, then the saying that is written will come true: "Death has been swallowed up in victory."
> [55] "Where, O death, is your victory?
> Where, O death, is your sting?"
> 1 Corinthians 15: 51-55

When the perishable has been clothed with the imperishable, and the mortal with immortality, then you will experience that Death has been swallowed up in victory. Where, O death, is your victory? Where, O death, is your sting? Suffering is transformed into peace.

THE WAY OF THE CROSS

Once again, I enjoy how Eckhart Tolle plays with this idea. He states, *There are many accounts of people who say they have found God through their deep suffering, and there is the Christian expression "the way of the cross," which I suppose points to the same thing.*[15] He goes on to say, *We are concerned with nothing else here. Strictly speaking, they did not find God through their suffering, because suffering implies resistance. They found God through surrender, through total acceptance of what is, into which they were forced by their intense suffering.*[16]

Eckhart has a problem here because, in reality, suffering leads you to open yourself to faith in God—God is Love. Love transforms.

> [1]Therefore, since we have been justified through faith, we have peace with God through our Lord Jesus Christ, [2] through whom we have gained access by faith into this grace in which we now stand. And we boast in the hope of the glory of God. [3] Not only so, but we also glory in our sufferings, because we know that suffering produces perseverance; [4] perseverance, character; and character, hope. [5] And hope does not

put us to shame, because God's love has been poured out into our hearts through the Holy Spirit, who has been given to us.
Romans 5: 1-5

Through suffering, faith is formed—you open to grace, the presence of the Holy Spirit. Perseverance, character, and hope are born. Love is poured out into your heart. Scripture is an amazing completion of Eckhart Tolle's message. *The Way of the Cross* leads to peace.

Scripture develops this message with exciting news: glorious strength is available, and power to grasp the depth of Love.

> [16] I pray that out of his glorious riches he may strengthen you with power through his Spirit in your inner Being, [17] so that Christ may dwell in your hearts through faith. And I pray that you, being rooted and established in love, [18] may have power, together with all the Lord's holy people, to grasp how wide and long and high and deep is the love of Christ, [19] and to know this love that surpasses knowledge—that

you may be filled to the measure of
all the fullness of God.
Ephesians 3: 16-19

Exciting, isn't it! Love's glorious riches strengthen you—empower you. Love's Holy Spirit indwells and leads. You are surrendered and at peace, knowing how wide and long and high and deep is the Love of Christ. As you open to Christ's Love, you avail yourself to be filled to the measure of all the fullness of God.

THE POWER TO CHOOSE
I was excited to read Eckhart Tolle's opening to this section, *The Power To Choose*. His ramblings about the word 'choice' open the door to some thoughts from Scripture. First, take a look at Eckhart Tolle's ramblings.

Choice implies consciousness—a high degree of consciousness. Without it, you have no choice. Choice begins the moment you disidentify from the mind and its conditioned patterns, the moment you become present. Until you reach that point, you are unconscious, spiritually speaking.[17]
The consciousness that he is referring to is an openness to the indwelling Holy Spirit. He is stating, you can have all of the mental

development and increased knowledge available, but unless it is *counterbalanced by the corresponding growth in consciousness, the potential for unhappiness and disaster is very great.*[18] What is he saying?

By consciousness, Eckhart Tolle is referring to your openness and attention to that inner nature—the indwelling voice. You can have all the knowledge and learning from the world, but if you do not have that interior presence, the knowledge and learning are empty. The choice is always present in every moment of life. What are you seeking? What are you asking? What door are you knocking on? Eckhart Tolle would be more accurate if he said your consciousness needs to be tuned to Love—the branch attached to the vine.

Many years ago, I was introduced to a mind set: 'Practice the Presence of God.' *The Practice of the Presence of God,*[19] is a book of collected teachings of Brother Lawrence (born Nicolas Herman), a Carmelite friar from the 17th century. The principle is quite simple.

You are always looking to acquire the presence of God—the presence of Love. Brother Lawrence's approach was to be always governed by Love, without selfish intent. His rule of life—being resolved to make Love the end of all his actions. In this he found satisfaction and peace.

In every action, washing dishes, sweeping the floor, greeting people, he did it for Love. He was not focusing on what he would gain, worldly value or identity, but seeking Love only, and nothing else. Brother Lawrence was always in the habit of conversing with Love continually. It is a relationship of interactiveness. All of life is valuable to Love, one does not need to accomplish great things. You are to be available to Love—Love created you for Love. That is practicing the presence of God! You are encouraged to start today.

Eckhart Tole misses the mark when he did not encourage you to practice the presence of God. This is the real *Power To Choose*.

THE LAST RECAPITULATION:
THE THESIS

Questions: What is your thesis? What is the context that you want your actions and words to reflect? What are the principles, guidelines, and actions you impose on your life to reach this desired thesis? How can your life be summed up in one or two sentences?

This is the challenge you face after reading these 240 some pages.

What have you learned from these pages, and how do you apply them in your life? You and all humanity want to be happy. As well, you and all of humanity want to rid yourselves of what Eckhart Tolle calls the pain-body. You all want to be whole in mind, body, soul, and spirit.

You are reminded of Love's promise in Jeremiah and Love's purpose for the indwelling Holy Spirit—Rivers of Living Water.

> [11] For I know the plans I have for you," declares the LORD, "plans to prosper you and not to harm you, plans to give you hope and a future. [12] Then you will call on me and come and pray to me, and I will listen to you. [13] You will seek me and find me when you seek me with all your heart. [14] I will be found by you," declares the LORD, "and will bring you back from captivity.[a] I will gather you from all the nations and places where I have banished you," declares the LORD, "and will bring

you back to the place from which I carried you into exile."
Jeremiah 29: 11-14
Footnotes
a. *will restore your fortunes*

These promises, this relationship with the indwelling Holy Spirit, will restore you, guide you to your fulfillment, and empower you, carrying and leading you through Love. The Rivers of Living Water heal, exhort, love, and bless. The Rivers are not static but a potentially tumultuous, explosive, Dunamis power.

Eckhart Tolle's mission is to provide you with the spiritual wisdom necessary to experience your connectedness with the miraculous world around you and to develop mastery of life. I have found that his wisdom is interesting but incomplete.

Let me explain. Scriptural teachings present the 'mysteries,' in the form of esoteric knowledge, of which Christ spoke in Matthew 13 and Luke 8.

> [11] He replied, "Because the knowledge of the secrets of the kingdom of heaven has been given to you, but not to them. [12] Whoever has will be given more, and they will

have an abundance. Whoever does not have, even what they have will be taken from them. ¹³ This is why I speak to them in parables: "Though seeing, they do not see; though hearing, they do not hear or understand. ¹⁴ In them is fulfilled the prophecy of Isaiah: "'You will be ever hearing but never understanding; you will be ever seeing but never perceiving. ¹⁵ For this people's heart has become calloused; they hardly hear with their ears, and they have closed their eyes. Otherwise they might see with their eyes, hear with their ears, understand with their hearts and turn, and I would heal them.' ¹⁶ But blessed are your eyes because they see, and your ears because they hear. ¹⁷ For truly I tell you, many prophets and righteous people longed to see what you see but did not see it, and to hear what you hear but did not hear it.
Matthew 13: 11-17
(Luke 8: 10)

In this passage Jesus is talking to His disciples. He is answering the question, "Why does He speak to the people in parables rather than teaching them through clear statements?"

The question spawns a few more questions. Who receives the mysteries, 'the secrets of the kingdom of heaven'? Who is offered the 'abundance'? Jesus explains that only those whose hearts are open to Him and believe in Him can understand the mysteries of the kingdom. Becoming a disciple of Christ Jesus and believing in Him are key to understanding and connecting with the Trinity: Father, Son, and Holy Spirit.

Jesus states that the knowledge of the secrets of God's Kingdom has been granted to the disciples, implying a special understanding and insight. Others hear the parable stories and teachings convey spiritual truths in a veiled way. Parables might be compared to thermometers; they reveal a person's spiritual condition. It is a reminder that understanding requires a receptive heart and a willingness to seek God's truth.

Your being a true disciple is not just being a student, searching and learning, but a follower who applies what you have learned.

I began this book by stating that I am writing a counter argument to *The Power of Now*, by the contemporary spiritual teacher Eckhart Tolle.

Throughout this book I have referenced his words and paired them with Scripture. In that comparison, Scripture always gives depth and substance to Eckhart Tolle's words. The exegesis of Scripture shows the truth of Jesus' statements and corrects Eckhart Tolle's New Age tendencies.

A summary from Scripture will provide the final depth, enabling you to see the path before you. It is a bit long and deep, but it will complete the idea being presented in this book. It is often titled "The Greatest Commandment."

> [28] One of the teachers of the law came and heard them debating. Noticing that Jesus had given them a good answer, he asked him, "Of all the commandments, which is the most important?" [29] "The most important one," answered Jesus, "is this: 'Hear, O Israel: The Lord our God, the Lord is one. [30] Love the Lord your God with all your heart and with all your soul and with all your mind and with all your strength.' [31] The second is this: 'Love your neighbor as yourself.' There is no commandment greater than these." [32] "Well said, teacher," the

man replied. "You are right in saying that God is one and there is no other but him. ³³ To love him with all your heart, with all your understanding and with all your strength, and to love your neighbor as yourself is more important than all burnt offerings and sacrifices." ³⁴ When Jesus saw that he had answered wisely, he said to him, "You are not far from the kingdom of God." And from then on no one dared ask him any more questions.
Mark 12: 28-34

The message of this book is that you are to Love the Lord your God with all your heart and with all your soul and with all your mind and with all your strength.

Your whole essence is to connect and be in relationship with God. At the beginning of the book, I referred to this essence as Love. God is Love and Love made you. You are an image of Love. Only Love can fill that hole inside you.

The Lord our God, the Lord is One. God, as you have read, is a Trinity of persons: Father,

Son, and Holy Spirit. They are 'One.' Jesus expressed this in a prayer to the Father in John 17: 21, *that all of them may be one, Father, just as you are in me and I am in you.* They are one, and we are to be one with them.

As you enter into Love, become one with the Father, Son, and Holy Spirit, you will experience the outflow: Love, Joy, Peace, Patience, Gentleness, and Self-Control—the Fruit of His Spirit. This same outflow, the Rivers of Living Water, will drive your ability to *Love your neighbor as yourself.* It is wonderful and mysterious.

You might also find yourself praying this prayer to the Father.

> Our Father, who art in heaven,
> hallowed be Thy name.
> Thy kingdom come; Thy will be done
> on earth as it is in heaven.

You are to be one with the Father, your Creator, the source of life. You are to invite His Kingdom to come to the Earth, to be here now. You are to enter into this presence, sharing it with those around you. As well, you are to enter into a relationship with His Spirit, the Holy Spirit, to be led by His will.

Let me remind you of the three words from Dr. Charles Stanley: Dependency, Sensitivity and Obedience. As you open in dependency to the Holy Spirit, you become more sensitive to His lead and more able to apply it to your life. This dependency and sensitivity lead to obedience. It is not forced. You have free will. As you follow the lead of the Holy Spirit, you are happier and have that peace that passes all understanding.

Let me suggest some simple practices! These practices are NOT going to tie you to me. I am directing you to look to the indwelling Holy Spirit; the Holy Spirit is the teacher, counsellor, healer, and spiritual guide who will lead you.

These practices stem from ancient, timeless, spiritual truths.

ANCIENT TIMELESS, SPIRITUAL TRUTHS

1. Practice the Presence – Commit yourself to Love and form a relationship with His Holy Spirit.

2. Ask for the Baptism in the Holy Spirit.

3. Take 10 minutes in the morning each day to read and muse on Scripture.

4. Each week take a principle from Scripture and practice it.

5. Join others who are practicing their Scriptural faith – walk with a community.

6. Reach out to those around you and share your faith in Jesus.

7. At the end of each day, review your day by asking two questions.

   - When was I closest to God today—closest to Love today?
   - When was I furthest away?

When you have an eternal perspective, you enjoy relationships and the things of the world. You are to live out of your dignity as a child of God—Love's child. Live with intentionality.

Enjoy the journey!

A PRAYER

> This prayer is used by permission from:
> Watkins, S.R., *Miracle Mornings, Volume 1; 31 Days of Declarations and Devotions,* Amazon/Kindle Direct Publishing, 2024. (Page 62).
> www.newstartministries.ca

You might end this journey through *The Power of Now is Love* by reflecting on this prayer:

Lord, I find myself woven intricately into Your design, blest by Your hand, and therefore, I am a conduit pipe of blessings unto others. Blessings come to me, and I pour them out to others. Each dawn, as the sun rises, I am reminded to count my blessings, to turn my gaze heavenward, and to offer gratitude to You, God, my Father, whose goodness knows no bounds. Your gentle mercies flow over my life, nurturing my soul and ensuring that goodness and grace blossom forth in abundance.

I ask You, Father God, to pour out Your grace, favour, and Your peace upon my family and I. Work wonders in our midst, O God. Reveal Your strength and Your glory in the land of the living. Let every knee bow, and every tongue confess, that Jesus Christ is Lord, the Alpha and the Omega, the Beginning and the End.

APPENDIX A —RIVERS OF LIVING WATER

> This material is taken from:
> Fabbi, Kenneth L., *Powered by the Gift of Tongues*. Kenneth L. Fabbi Publications, Lethbridge, Alberta, 2023, (Page 19).

Accessing the Rivers of Living Waters:

> [37] On the last and greatest day of the festival, Jesus stood and said in a loud voice, "Let anyone who is thirsty come to me and drink. [38] Whoever believes in me, as Scripture has said, rivers of living water will flow from within them." [39] By this he meant the Spirit, whom those who believed in him were later to receive. Up to that time the Spirit had not been given, since Jesus had not yet been glorified.
> John 7: 37-39

Up to this point the Holy Spirit was only seen on and through significant figures in the Old Testament, such as the prophets, like Moses and King David. In the New Testament Jesus explains that when He is glorified, the Father will send the Spirit. The Holy Spirit is the Gift from God the Father. Then, and only then, will you be able to access the 'rivers of living waters.' These rivers will flow from within you, from within your body, the Temple of God.

Did you notice that Scripture refers to accessing the 'Rivers,' not one river but many 'Rivers of Living Water'? It is not a little gurgling stream or trickling brook. It is a river, and not just a river but rivers. In other words, there is an endless supply: 'Let anyone who is thirsty come to me and drink.' All you have to do is believe, 'Whoever believes in me, as Scripture has said, rivers of living water will flow from within them.'

How are you going to get the Rivers of Living Water flowing from within? John's Scripture says, 'Let anyone who is thirsty come to me and drink,' and that 'living waters will flow from within them'—from their belly, from within.

How are you going to get this living water flowing? You get this living water flowing by praising God and by praying in Tongues! You open to the Spirit by praising God and activating your Tongues, which in turn activates the rivers of living water.

How much of this living water do you want? If you pray for a minute, you get a minute's worth. If you pray for an hour, you get an hour's worth. But what if you praised God or prayed in Tongues all day, every day?

You are to be charged up! You are to transform the world around you, like salt and yeast. You accomplish this by spending time praising God or praying in Tongues; praying for your brothers and sisters in Christ, praying for issues, praying about your neighbor that bothers you, and praying for protection for your children.

Tongues is a wonderful tool! Do you know how to open the gates of Heaven? Pray in the Spirit! Tongues opens the spiritual realm. It opens you to its mysteries.

> [2] For anyone who speaks in a tongue does not speak to people but to God. Indeed, no one understands them; they utter mysteries by the Spirit.
> 1 Corinthians 14: 2

God the Holy Spirit, through this gift that you activate, is using your voice to praise God. As you come to use it, you become more connected, more in tune, and more alive in Him.

There is a River of Living Water inside your belly. This River of Living Water is like an atomic bomb that is available anytime you need to release it. It is available to you anytime you need it.

By praising God and by praying in Tongues you are releasing the Rivers of Living Water within you, which proclaim the things of God. The Rivers of Living Water heal, exhort, love, and bless. It is not a static event but a potentially tumultuous, explosive, Dunamis power. Tongues open you up to God's mysteries.

Did you know that everything God has for you is a blessing? The more you apprehend from His Holy Spirit, the more you release the Rivers of Living Water, the more you are communing with God, and the more you will feel the Fruit of His Spirit—Love, Joy, Peace, Patience, Gentleness, and Self-Control (Galatians 5: 22-23).

Do you need more Love? Praise God or pray in Tongues! Do you need more Joy? Praise God or pray in Tongues! Do you need more Peace, Patience, Gentleness and Self-Control? Praise God or pray in Tongues!

¹⁶ Rejoice always, ¹⁷ pray continually, ¹⁸ give thanks in all circumstances; for this is God's will for you in Christ Jesus.
1 Thessalonians 5: 16-18

Praising God or praying in Tongues empowers you, the believer, uniting you like a branch to the vine.

It's all about Love

APPENDIX B
—THE EXCHANGE AT THE CROSS

> This material is taken from:
> Fabbi, Kenneth L. *Five Fold Cycle Workbook – Method of Healing Personal Hurt,* Kenneth Fabbi Publications, Lethbridge, Alberta, 2024. (Page 8.)

If you have a need or problem in your life, there is only one place and one place alone where you must go to find the provision or God's solution. And that one place is the Cross of Jesus.

Through what Jesus accomplished by His death on the Cross, every provision of God for you; spiritual, physical, material, for time or eternity, has been made available.

There is no other basis than the Cross for all the provision of God.

It is through the Cross and through the Cross only that you can come to God and receive His provisions and His blessings.

In order to do that, you need to understand the basic nature of what took place when Jesus died on the Cross. At that point a 'divinely ordained exchange' took place. Ordained by God and predicted many centuries before by the Prophets of Israel.

The Exchange is all summed up in one key verse of the prophet Isaiah 53.

> We all, like sheep, have gone astray each of us has turned to our own way; and the LORD has laid on him the iniquity of us all.
> Isaiah 53: 6

That is the absolute center of all that God has to offer for you. It is entirely the grace of God. You have no claim upon God; you could not have demanded this from God, but in His infinite grace and mercy, God ordained this exchange.

Simply: God laid on Jesus the iniquity of us all. (Iniquity could also be translated 'rebellion.' Rebellion and all the consequences and judgments that come upon rebellion.)

Your rebellion, the rebellion of the entire sin-cursed Adamic race, came upon Jesus upon the Cross, by divine appointment.

That is the negative part of the exchange. The positive side is that in return, all the good that was due to the sinless obedience of Jesus might be available to you. God visited upon Jesus the evil due to you, that in return

He might make available to you the good due to Jesus.

Simply: The evil came upon Jesus so that the good might be available to you.

Now there is no claim upon God; you could not have demanded this from God, but in His infinite grace and mercy, God ordained this exchange.

God visited upon Jesus your rebellion, and then He endured all the evil consequences of your rebellion, which by justice should have come upon you.

The Cross was a divinely ordained exchange.

The evil came upon Jesus, that the good might be offered to you.

A FEW ASPECTS OF THIS EXCHANGE

Jesus was punished that you might be forgiven.

> [23] For the wages of sin is death, but the gift of God is eternal life in Christ Jesus our Lord.
> Romans 6: 23

Jesus bore your sins in His own body on the tree, that you, having died to sins, might live for righteousness.

Jesus was physically wounded that you might be physically healed.

> "He himself bore our sins" in his body on the cross, so that we might die to sins and live for righteousness; "by his wounds you have been healed."
> 1 Peter 2: 24; Isaiah 53: 4–6

What Jesus endured physically (wounding with whip, crown of thorns, spit, lance, carrying the cross, and hanging on the cross), He did so that you might be physically healed.

Jesus was made sin that you might be made righteous.

> God made him who had no sin to be sin for us, so that in him we might become the righteousness of God.
> 2 Corinthians 5: 21

Jesus was punished that you might be forgiven. He endured the judgment and punishment due to your rebellion so that, in Jesus, you become right before God the Father.

Jesus experiences death that you might receive eternal life.

> But we do see Jesus, who was made lower than the angels for a little while, now crowned with glory and honor because he suffered death, so that by the grace of God he might taste death for everyone. Hebrews 2: 9

What is the exchange? The Exchange is that Jesus experienced death that you might share His eternal life. This is redemption.

On the Cross Jesus endured your poverty. He was stripped. He was left totally impoverished. He was left with nothing. He took your poverty that you might share His abundance (2 Corinthians 8: 9).

On the Cross Jesus was rejected by God the Father. He cried out, and there came no answer from Heaven. He died of a broken heart, a heart broken by rejection, but by His rejection you have acceptance by God the Father (Matthew 27: 46).

The truth in Scripture is repeated time and time again—evil came on Jesus that the good might be available to you.

Jesus becomes a curse that you might receive the blessing.

Paul says:

> [13] Christ redeemed us from the curse of the law by becoming a curse for us, for it is written: "Cursed is everyone who is hung on a pole." [14] He redeemed us in order that the blessing given to Abraham might come to the Gentiles through Christ Jesus, so that by faith we might receive the promise of the Spirit.
> Galatians 3: 13-14

This Scripture explains the exchange that was foretold in Deuteronomy 21: 23 of the Old Testament, 'Cursed is everyone who hangs on a tree.'

In the exchange it is obvious: the evil is the curse and the good is the blessing.

The words "bless" or "blessing" occur in the Bible approximately 430 times. The word "curse" in various forms occurs in the Bible approximately 160 times.

Jesus had to become a curse that you might be redeemed from the curse and receive the blessing.

What was exchanged?

Galatians 3: 13-14 – Jesus becomes a curse, that you might receive the blessing.

1 Peter 2: 24 – By His wounds you are healed.

Matthew 8: 17 – He took your infirmities and bore your diseases.

2 Corinthians 5: 21 – Jesus is made sin so that you receive righteousness.

Hebrews 2: 9 – He suffers death, that you might receive life.

Isaiah 53: 4-6 – All your inequity is laid on Him, that you might be whole.

Hebrews 9: 15 – He is the Mediator of a New Covenant that you may receive eternal life.

Hebrews 9: 24-28 – By His Sacrifice He removed sin once and for all.

Hebrews 10: 10 – By the offering of His body, you have been sanctified once for all.

Romans 6: 23 – Jesus was punished that you might be forgiven.

2 Corinthians 8: 9 – Jesus took your poverty that you might share His abundance.

Matthew 27: 46 – Jesus was rejected by God the Father that you might have acceptance.

Christ is the mediator of a new covenant - once and for all!
1 Timothy 2: 5

The Exchange material can be obtained through: Derek Prince Ministries of Canada, Suite #178, 111 Davis Drive, Unit 23, Newmarket, Ontario, L3Y 9E5. Phone: 1-647-217-8923

APPENDIX C
– FIVE FOLD CYCLE
– METHOD OF HEALING PERSONAL HURT

> This material is taken from:
> Fabbi, Kenneth L., *Five Fold Cycle – Method of Healing Personal Hurt: Healing Life's Hurts,* Kenneth Fabbi Publications, Lethbridge, Alberta, Third Printing, 2019.

The Five Fold Cycle – Diagram

METHOD OF HEALING PERSONAL HURT

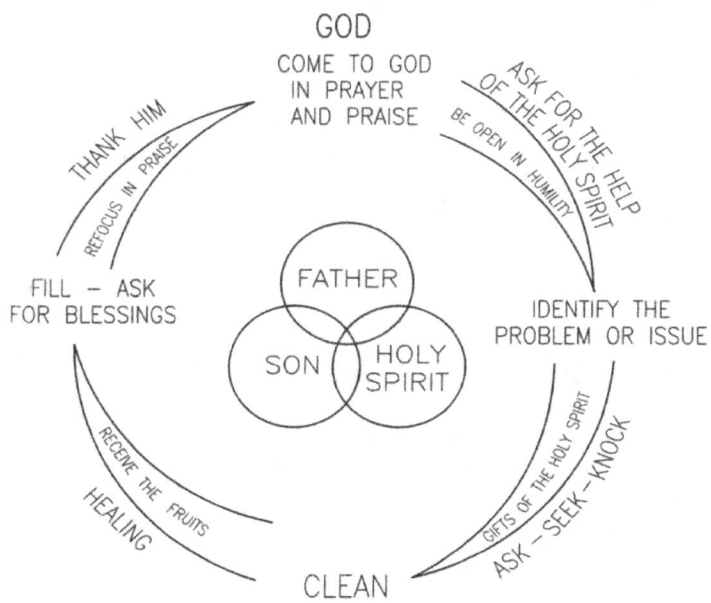

The Five Fold Cycle

— Method Of Healing
Personal Hurt

(A PROBLEM SOLVING METHOD)

I train people to do personal housecleaning. It goes like this:

When we are hurt, there are 3 negative reactions:

1. Unforgiveness - Anger, bitterness, resentment and the like are the first major problem.

2. Guilt - which is self-pity, uncertainty, not forgiving self, worry, anxiety, tension caused by worry is the second problem.

3. Depression - This is a symptom of the previous two and therefore when you deal with #1 and #2, depression leaves on its own.

Process:

The answer to how to deal with these is easy if you believe in Christ's help. It goes through a *Five Fold Cycle*.

> **1. Become God Focused:** Focus on God in prayer praise and thanksgiving. Ask for the gifts of the Spirit, which include wisdom, knowledge and understanding. Be humble and penitent.
>
> **2. Identify:** Identify problems and be specific. Ask for wisdom and knowledge from the Lord. Look for specific sources for the problems and expand on them. Often problems interconnect, so make sure to separate and individualize them. Do things one at a time. It is a process of healing.

3. Clean: Do something.

C
L
E
A
N
S
E

- Forgive where forgiveness is needed.
- Forgive others, God and self.
- Bind any spiritual involvement.
- Confess and ask for cleansing.
- Give up the problem to the Lord, e.g.: anxiety/ worry / etc.
- Ask the Lord to take it away.
- It is often important to actually follow through by personal contact with the parties involved. Be sensitive to the Lord's direction in this matter.
- It is good to take these matters to the Communion Table and repeat the process.

What we are doing in this section is gradually nibbling away at the problem areas. Remember you cannot deal with depression because it is a symptom and often very global in nature.

B
L
E
S
S
I
N
G

4. Fill:

- Ask for the in-filling of the Holy Spirit.
- Ask for the contrasting good characteristics.
- Ask for the blessings and gifts to fill the space left when you cleansed yourself in # 3.
- Prayer and Scripture reading are important.
- Make sure to ask for blessings for others. They also need the gifts and blessings.
- Ask the Lord to heal the hurt.
- Take it to Communion or Eucharist.

If you clean the areas/problems and do nothing to replace them with positives, there is a high probability that you can slip back into the same old routines. You must fill the place that has been cleaned up, with the good things from God through his Holy Spirit.

5. Thank the Lord:
Go back to # 1. Stop focusing on yourself. Thank the Lord.

APPENDIX D
—BAPTISM IN THE HOLY SPIRIT

> This material is taken from:
> Fabbi, Kenneth L. *Five Fold Cycle Workbook – Method of Healing Personal Hurt,* Kenneth Fabbi Publications, Lethbridge, Alberta, 2024. (Page 130.)

What is Baptism in the Spirit? Is it different than Baptism? Is it different from what they call Confirmation in the mainline churches?

Baptism of the Holy Spirit comes when the Holy Spirit, already residing in you from the time you accepted Jesus as Savior, is released to operate fully in your lives. As Dennis Bennett used to say, the question is not, "Do you have the Holy Spirit?" But rather, "Does the Holy Spirit have you?"

From the day of His conception, the Holy Spirit resided in Jesus. There was never a moment in His life when He was not God. Yet, for the first 30 years of His life, there is no recorded ministry of Jesus, other than those occasions when He was found in the temple as a young boy (Luke 2: 41-52). Except for the wedding feast at Cana (John 2: 1-12), there are no recorded teachings or miracles —not until He was baptized in the Jordan at the hands of John the Baptist. This was the event in Jesus' life where the Holy Spirit was released to empower His ministry.

So, what happened to Him at the River Jordan? John says Jesus was baptized in the Holy Spirit.

> Then John gave this testimony: "I saw the Spirit come down from heaven as a dove and remain on him.
> John 1: 32

His disciples also had an experience at Pentecost (Acts 2: 1-4), where they were empowered by the Holy Spirit to heal, teach, and lead people to a closer relationship with God.

When the Holy Spirit is released in your lives, you discover it is possible to live the way God expects you to live, and His power affects every area of your lives. Listening to God's Spirit is essential for healing.

Must everyone be baptized in the Holy Spirit? Jesus said,

> If you then, though you are evil, know how to give good gifts to your children, how much more will your Father in heaven give the Holy Spirit to those who ask him!"
> Luke 11: 13

From this you understand that the Holy Spirit is available to everyone.

The Baptism in the Spirit is a release of the Spirit, usually occurring with the realization that there is a potential available that you have not activated. People may well have been Baptized and received Confirmation, but never enter into an inter-active relationship with the Holy Spirit. It is like receiving a wrapped gift and putting it on the mantle. You have received it, but you have not opened the box and activated the gifts and fruit of the Holy Spirit.

RECEIVING THE HOLY SPIRIT
\- - -
BAPTISM IN THE HOLY SPIRIT

> This material is taken from:
> Fabbi, Kenneth L. *Five Fold Cycle Workbook – Method of Healing Personal Hurt,* Kenneth Fabbi Publications, Lethbridge, Alberta, 2024. (Appendix G)

This is the Gift from God the Father that Jesus referred to in Luke 24:

> [48] You are witnesses of these things. [49] I am going to send you what my Father has promised; but stay in the city until you have been clothed with power from on high."
> Luke 24: 48-49

PRAYER FOR THE BAPTISM IN THE SPIRIT

(If you have never been Baptized in the Holy Spirit, you might pray these prayers.)

READY YOURSELF
Take a moment to calm yourself, close your eyes, clear your mind, and become quiet before the Lord.

1. PRAYER FOR EXPECTANT FAITH
Lord, give me now a deeper faith and trust in you. Deepen my faith, Lord. Help me to cling to you closer than ever before. I believe, Lord, that you love me and want to touch me.

2. PRAYER FOR REPENTANT HEART
Heavenly Father, in your presence and in the presence of my brothers and sisters, I acknowledge my sins. I repent of my evil ways and ask for your mercy. In the power of the blood of Jesus purify me and cleanse me. I firmly resolve with your help never to sin again and to avoid whatever leads to sin in the name of Jesus, have mercy on me.

3. PRAYER FOR A FORGIVING HEART
Heavenly Father, as you have forgiven me, so ought I to forgive those who hurt me. From the depth of my heart I forgive and release to you_____.
(This is a time to forgive and release those who have hurt you in the past. A time to open your heart to God, your Father.)

4. DELIVERANCE PRAYER
(As adopted children, we receive the right to pray against evil from our Baptism.)
In the name of Jesus, I take authority over any evil spirits who may be oppressing me. I bind you, evil spirits, and I command you in the name of Jesus to be silent. I seal you off from my woundedness and hurts and emotions. In the power of the blood of Jesus, I now break any seal you may have on me. In the name of Jesus, son of the father, son of the virgin Mary, I command you to leave now and go to Jesus to be disposed of according to his will.

5. PRAYER FOR HEALING

Lord JESUS, you alone know the areas in my spirit that need healing. Let your love now flow in. In the power of your precious blood, heal me.

6. ACCEPTING JESUS AS LORD

Lord Jesus, I accept you as my personal Lord and Savior. I place you on the throne of my life. I surrender my life to you. From now on I belong to you. I want to walk in your ways and under your Lordship all the days of my life.

7. YIELDING TO THE BAPTISM IN THE SPIRIT

Lord Jesus, now I am ready. I have emptied myself, repented of my sins, and proclaimed you as my personal Lord and Savior. I ask you to fill me with the living waters of your Spirit. I claim the promise you made: if we ask, we will receive. I am now asking Lord in faith. Come Holy Spirit and baptize me.

8. PRAYER FOR THE GIFT OF TONGUES

Holy Spirit please release in me now the Gift of Tongues. I surrender my gift of speech to you so that you may enrich me with a personal prayer gift. Holy Spirit, accept the syllables I now utter _____.

(You might focus on the Lord and repeat the word 'ABBA.') (Often it is best to close your eyes and simply hum or sing a simple melody to the Lord, waiting on the melody to change into Tongues.)

9. PRAYER FOR THE GIFTS

Holy Spirit please give me all the other gifts that you see fit so that I may be equipped to lead a full Christian life and be of service to the community. I ask you, Lord, to enrich me with the gifts of Word of Wisdom, Word of Knowledge, Faith, Healing, Miracles, Prophecy, Discernment of Spirits, Public Tongues, and Interpretation.

10. THANKSGIVING PRAYER

Thank you, Jesus, for baptizing me in your Holy Spirit. To you be the glory.

APPENDIX E
—THE ART OF FORGIVENESS

> This material is taken from:
> Roycroft, Thomas W. & Kenneth L. Fabbi. *You Can Minister Spiritual Gifts,* Kenneth Fabbi, Canada, 2019. (Page 88.)

In the process of forgiveness there are 4 steps: a decision to forgive, repentance and release of the hurt, the act of forgiving self and others, and finally asking God's blessing on the situation.

PRACTICAL STEPS TO FORGIVENESS

1) Make a decision to forgive.

  –Forgiveness is not a feeling.
  –Forgiveness is not an emotion.
  –Forgiveness is a decision.

2) Repent and release the hurt.

   −Hurt can be described as hatred, bitterness, and resentment.
   −These are doors to evil spirits.
   −Close the doors to evil.
   −Release the hurt to the Cross of Jesus.

3) Forgive God, yourself, and others!

4) Ask God's blessing on the other person, a blessing on yourself, and a blessing on the situation.

───────────────────────────────

PRAYER FOR A FORGIVING HEART

> This material is taken from:
> Fabbi, Kenneth L. *Five Fold Cycle Workbook – Method of Healing Personal Hurt,* Kenneth Fabbi Publications, Lethbridge, Alberta, 2024. (Page 23.)

Father, I ask You to take judgment and bitterness out of my life.

I forgive *(Fill in the blank.)* _____ _____ for hurting me.

I do not want this in my life—I repent and ask You to remove it. Heal my heart—forgive my sin.

I receive your forgiveness.

Father, forgive my anger, resentment, bitterness, and unforgiveness.

From this day forward, I resolve not to judge others, and I put their actions on the Cross. I place *(Fill in the blank.)* _____ into your hands.

I proclaim my trust in You alone, my God. You are the Righteous Judge.

Father, bless _____ in every way.

In Jesus, I thank you, Father. Amen.

FOOTNOTES:

INTRODUCTION

[1] Eckhart Tolle —Eckhart Tolle is a German-born spiritual teacher and self-help author.

While working toward his doctorate at the University of Cambridge in 1977, Tolle abandoned his studies after a claimed spiritual awakening and later began working as a spiritual teacher. He came to prominence as a self-help author beginning in the 2000s, aided through promotion by Oprah Winfrey. His teachings draw from traditions such as Zen Buddhism, Christian mysticism, Sufism, and Hinduism, although he remains unaffiliated with any religion.

Eckhart Tolle. (2025, August 4). In Wikipedia. https://en.wikipedia.org/wiki/Eckhart_Tolle

[2] Tolle, Eckhart., *The Power of Now: A Guide to Spiritual Enlightenment*, Namaste Publishing, Vancouver, B.C. and New World Library, Novato, CA.,1999.
[3] ibid 9.
[4] ibid 8.
[5] ibid 9.

Chapter One
[1] ibid 13.
[2] ibid 13.

[3] ibid 15.
[4] ibid Back Cover.
[5] Dr Masaru Emoto water experiment)
Emoto, Masaru, *The Hidden Messages in Water*, Atria Books, N.Y., 2008. (https://masaru-emoto.net/)
[6] Mike Ensley, Jun 13, 2022, *Emotional Entanglement*, Comeback Story Counseling, https://www.nocostory.com/post/emotional-entanglement
[7] *Quantum Entanglement.* (2025, August 10). In Wikipedia. https://en.wikipedia.org/wiki/Quantum_entanglement
[8] Tolle 17.
[9] ibid 17.
[10] Jesus came to be called "Jesus Christ" (meaning "Jesus the *Khristós*", i.e. "Jesus the Messiah" or "Jesus the Anointed") by Christians, who believe that his crucifixion and resurrection fulfill the messianic prophecies of the Old Testament, especially the prophecies outlined in Isaiah 53 and Psalm 22.
Christ (title). (2025, August 20). In Wikipedia. https://en.wikipedia.org/wiki/Christ_(title)#:~:text=Jesus%20came%20to%20be%20called,Isaiah%2053%20and%20Psalm%2022.
[11] ibid 21.
[12] ibid 21.
[13] ibid 25.
[14] ibid 25.
[15] ibid 25.

[16] Fabbi. Kenneth L., *Five Fold Cycle – Method of Healing Personal Hurt: Healing Life's Hurts,* Lethbridge, Alberta, Canada, Kenneth L. Fabbi, 2019.
[17] Tolle 29.
[18] ibid 29.
[19] ibid 29.
[20] Fabbi, Kenneth L., *Scripture Healing: How to Play Pray Scripture,* Kenneth L. Fabbi Publications, Lethbridge, Alberta, 2019
[21] Tolle 31.

Chapter Two
[1] Tolle 32.
[2] ibid 33.
[3] ibid 33.
[4] ibid 35.
[5] ibid 35.
[6] ibid 36.
[7] ibid 37.
[8] ibid 37.
[9] ibid 39.
[10] ibid 39.
[11] ibid Back Cover.
[12] ibid 41.
[13] ibid 42.
[14] ibid Back Cover.
[15] ibid 43.
[16] ibid 43.
[17] ibid 44.
[18] ibid 45.
[19] ibid 45.

[20] ibid 46.

Chapter Three
[1] Tolle 47.
[2] ibid 47.
[3] ibid 48.
[4] ibid 48.
[5] ibid 49.
[6] ibid 51.
[7] ibid 51.
[8] ibid 52.
[9] ibid 53.
[10] ibid 54.
[11] ibid 55.
[12] ibid 56.
[13] Tolle 56.
[14] ibid 57.
[15] ibid 57.
[16] ibid 61.
[17] ibid 61.
[18] ibid 62.
[19] ibid 63.
[20] Dr. Charles Stanley (1932-2023) was a Pastor Emeritus of First Baptist Church in Atlanta, Georgia, where he served as senior pastor for 49 years. He was the founder and president of In Touch Ministries as he broadcasts his sermons through television and radio.
[21] Tolle 64.
[22] ibid 64.
[23] ibid 65.
[24] ibid 65.

[25] ibid 67.
[26] ibid 67.
[27] ibid 67.
[28] ibid 68.
[29] ibid 69.
[30] ibid 70.

Chapter Four
[1] Tolle 73.
[2] ibid 73.
[3] ibid 73-74.
[4] ibid 75.
[5] ibid 76.
[6] ibid 77.
[7] ibid 77.
[8] ibid 77.
[9] ibid 77.
[10] ibid 79.
[11] ibid 79.
[12] ibid 80.
[13] ibid 82.
[14] ibid 82.
[15] ibid 83.
[16] ibid 83.
[17] ibid 83.
[18] ibid 84.
[19] ibid 85.
[20] ibid 85.
[21] ibid 87.
[22] ibid 87.
[23] ibid 88.
[24] ibid 88.

[25] ibid 88.
[26] ibid 89.
[27] ibid 90.
[28] ibid 90-91.
[29] ibid 91.
[30] ibid 91.
[31] ibid 91.

Chapter Five
[1] Tolle 94.
[2] ibid 94.
[3] ibid 95.
[4] ibid 96.
[5] ibid 96.
[6] ibid 97.
[7] ibid 98.
[8] ibid 99.
[9] ibid 99.
[10] ibid 100.
[11] ibid 100.
[12] Charles John Ellicott, 1878-1883, *Ephesians,* Bible Commentaries *Studylight.org,* https://www.studylight.org/commentaries/eng/ebc/ephesians.html .
[13] Tolle 103.
[14] ibid 104.
[15] Tolle, Eckhart., 1977, Personal Awakening, https://eckharttolle.com/personal-awakening.

Chapter Six
[1] Fabbi. Kenneth L., *Five Fold Cycle – Method of Healing Personal Hurt: Healing Life's Hurts,* Lethbridge, Alberta, Canada, Kenneth L. Fabbi, 2019.
[2] Tolle 108.
[3] ibid 108.
[4] ibid 109.
[5] ibid 110.
[6] ibid 111.
[7] ibid 111.
[8] ibid 111.
[9] ibid 112.
[10] ibid 113.
[11] ibid 113.
[12] ibid 114.
[13] ibid 115.
[14] ibid 115.
[15] ibid 115.
[16] ibid 115.
[17] Wikipedia, December, 2020, De (Chinese), Wikipedia.org. https://en.wikipedia.org/wiki/De_(Chinese)#
[18] Tolle 116.
[19] ibid 118.
[20] ibid 118.
[21] ibid 119.
[22] ibid 119.
[23] ibid 120.
[24] ibid 120.
[25] ibid 121.

[26] ibid 122.
[27] ibid Back Cover.
[28] ibid 122-123.
[29] ibid 123.
[30] ibid 123.
[31] ibid 123.
[32] ibid 124.
[33] ibid 124.
[34] ibid 125.
[35] ibid 125-126.
[36] ibid 126.
[37] ibid 126-127
[38] ibid 127.
[39] ibid 127.

Chapter Seven
[1] Tolle 129.
[2] ibid 130.
[3] ibid 131.
[4] ibid 131.
[5] ibid 132.
[6] ibid 133-134.
[7] ibid 134.
[8] ibid 134.
[9] ibid 135.
[10] ibid 135.
[11] ibid Back Cover.
[12] ibid 136.
[13] ibid 136.
[14] ibid 137.
[15] ibid 139.
[16] ibid 140.

[17] ibid 140.
[18] ibid 141.
[19] ibid 141.
[20] ibid 141-142.
[21] ibid 142.
[22] ibid 142.
[23] ibid 143.
[24] ibid 143.
[25] ibid Back Cover

Chapter Eight
[1] Tolle 145.
[2] ibid 145.
[3] ibid 145.
[4] ibid 146.
[5] ibid 147.
[6] ibid 148.
[7] ibid 149.
[8] ibid 150.
[9] ibid 150.
[10] ibid 150.
[11] ibid 152.
[12] ibid 152.
[13] ibid 152-153.
[14] ibid 153-154.
[15] ibid 154.
[16] ibid 154.
[17] ibid 155.
[18] ibid 157.
[19] ibid 157.
[20] ibid 158.
[21] ibid 160.

[22] ibid 160.
[23] ibid 161.
[24] ibid 163.
[25] ibid 164.
[26] ibid 165.
[27] ibid 165.
[28] ibid 166.
[29] Bordwell, David., *Catechism of the Catholic Church*, Continuum International Publishing, 2002, page 84
[30] Tolle 166.
[31] ibid 166.
[32] ibid 167.
[33] ibid 167.
[34] ibid 168.
[35] ibid 172.
[36] ibid 172.
[37] ibid 173.
[38] ibid 174.
[39] ibid 174.
[40] ibid 174.

Chapter Nine
[1] Tolle 178.
[2] ibid 178.
[3] ibid 178.
[4] ibid 178.
[5] ibid 178.
[6] ibid 179.
[7] ibid 180.
[8] ibid 180-181.
[9] ibid 182.

[10] ibid 182.
[11] ibid 183.
[12] ibid 183.
[13] ibid 186.
[14] ibid 187.
[15] ibid 188-189.
[16] ibid 189.
[17] ibid 189-190.
[18] ibid 192.
[19] ibid 195.
[20] ibid 196.
[21] ibid 196.
[22] ibid 197.
[23] ibid 201.
[24] ibid 201.
[25] ibid 201.

Chapter Ten
[1] Tolle 205.
[2] ibid 205.
[3] ibid 208.
[4] ibid 208.
[5] ibid 210.
[6] ibid 211.
[7] Fabbi, Kenneth L., *Five Fold Cycle Workbook – Method of Healing Personal Hurt*, Kenneth L. Fabbi Publishing, Lethbridge, Alberta, 2024.
[8] Tolle 213.
[9] ibid 215.
[10] ibid 215.
[11] ibid 217.
[12] ibid 218.

[13] ibid 219-220.
[14] ibid 220-221.
[15] ibid 223.
[16] ibid 223-224.
[17] ibid 224.
[18] ibid 226.
[19] ibid 227.
[20] Brother Lawrence, *The Practice of the Presence of God,* Spire Books, Fleming H. Revell Co., Old Tappan, New Jersey, 1958.

KENNETH L. FABBI PUBLICATIONS

FIVE FOLD CYCLE –
Method of Healing Personal Hurt
Sub-titled: *Heal Life's Hurts*

February 28, 2019 - Third Publication

Five Fold Cycle teaches how to pray for Inner Healing and empowers people to pray and watch for God's healing in their lives and in the lives of people around them.
  Hard Cover ISBN: 978-0-9952039-0-7
  Paperback ISBN: 978-0-9952039-1-4
  eBook ISBN: 978-0-9952039-2-1
  Spanish Paperback ISBN: 978-0-9952039-7-6
  Spanish eBook ISBN: 978-0-9952039-8-3

YOU CAN MINISTER SPIRITUAL GIFTS
Original by Thomas W. Roycroft

It was re-published: March 02, 2019

Both this book and the previous book are good teaching tools. Prayer Group members and I re-edit Thomas W. Roycroft's material. He developed the book as a course on the gifts of the Holy Spirit, encouraging people to activate the gifts and live a life in God's Holy Ghost.
  Paperback ISBN: 978-0-9952039-3-8
  eBook ISBN: 978-0-9952039-4-5

SCRIPTURE HEALING:
How to ~~Play~~ Pray Scripture

It was published: August, 2019

Scripture Healing: How to ~~Play~~ Pray Scripture became a publishing project because Kenneth found truth in the fact that the Word of God Heals!

People who apply scripture to their life and pray with scripture get healed. As we read and take the Scripture into our mind and heart, God the Father uses it to transform us.

This booklet is meant to walk you through a collection of Scriptures from the Holy Bible. Each Scripture offers a truth. Many of the Scriptural passages offer insight into healing and God's design.

Kenneth encourages you to play and experiment with these ideas and share them with your friends.

    Paperback ISBN: 978-0-9952039-5-2
    eBook ISBN: 978-0-9952039-6-9
    Spanish Paperback ISBN: 978-0-9952039-9-0
    Spanish eBook ISBN: 978-1-7771066-0-7

POWERED BY THE GIFT OF TONGUES

It was published: September, 2023.

God the Father wants to give you his Holy Spirit (Luke 11: 13 & 2 Corinthians 5: 5). The Father's gift is *one gift,* and that is the Holy Spirit. In the Spirit reside many manifestations, Tongues being one of them. St. Paul makes it clear that it is desirable to have the Gift of Tongues: *"I would like everyone of you to speak in tongues..."* (1 Corinthians 13: 5). The conclusion that we can draw is that Christians should be asking our Father for His gift.

  Paperback ISBN: 978-1-7771066-1-4
  eBook ISBN: 978-1-7771066-2-1

FIVE FOLD CYCLE WORKBOOK –
Method of Healing Personal Hurt

It was published: May 13, 2024.

The Workbook expands the original text and outlines a Method of Healing Personal Hurt through the *Five Fold Cycle*. Through Scripture Studies, Study Notes and Workshops, students learn and implement the healing process, learning to open to God, listen to the Holy Spirit and receive the healing available through Jesus' death on the Cross.

  Paperback ISBN: 978-1-7771066-3-8
  eBook ISBN: 978-1-7771066-4-5

WHOLENESS THROUGH HEALING AND FORGIVENESS

It was published: December 2024.

Wholeness through Healing and Forgiveness offers two powerful prayers that will release emotional burdens and deepen your relationship with the Lord.

Rooted in biblical teachings, this booklet invites you to embark on a transformative journey of forgiveness, healing past wounds, and releasing God's extravagant healing love.

Discover the joy and peace that come from surrendering your hurts to God and allowing His love to renew your spirit.

  Paperback ISBN: 978-1-7771066-5-2
  eBook ISBN: 978-1-7771066-6-9

---

www.ingramcontent.com/pod-product-compliance
Lightning Source LLC
Chambersburg PA
CBHW071953070526
44583CB00015B/1171